READING AND WRITING Sourcebook

Authors
Robert Pavlik
Richard G. Ramsey

Great Source Education Group
a Houghton Mifflin Company
Wilmington, Massachusetts
www.greatsource.com

Authors

Richard G. Ramsey is currently a national educational consultant for many schools throughout the country and serves as President of Ramsey's Communications. For more than twenty-three years he has served as a teacher and a principal for grades 1–12. Dr. Ramsey has also served on the Curriculum Frameworks Committee for the State of Florida. A lifelong teacher and educator and former principal, he is now a nationally known speaker on improving student achievement and motivating students.

Robert Pavlik taught high school English and reading for seven years. His university assignments in Colorado and Wisconsin have included teaching secondary/content area reading, chairing a Reading/Language Arts Department, and directing a Reading/Learning Center. He is an author of several books and articles and serves as the Director of the School Design and Development Center at Marquette University.

Table of Contents

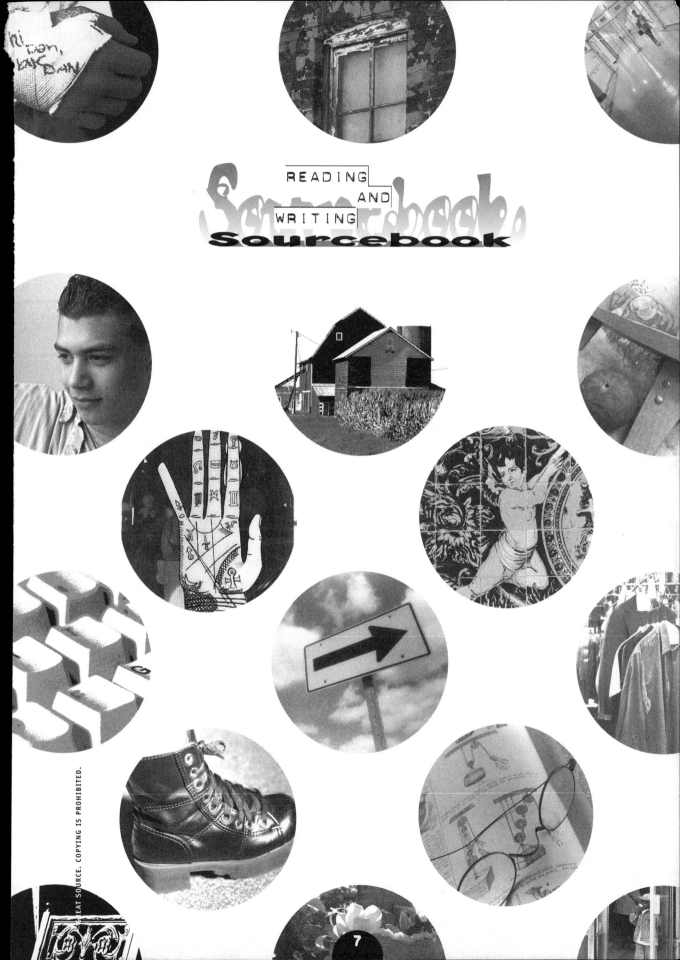

READING AND WRITING
Sourcebook

What's that? Say that again? We often ask others to repeat things we don't hear clearly. Often the same thing happens when we read. We don't understand everything the first time through. That's one reason why it helps to read with a pen in hand, marking lines of text, circling words, underlining phrases, and asking questions in the margins. It's easy to do, and it will help you understand more of what you read.

Read this brief and moving speech. Then look at the way the passage has been marked up by a reader.

RESPONSE NOTES

CLARIFY

He means "Surrender."

MARK

no food

VISUALIZE

Reasons
chiefs
young men
look for children

REACT

Moving!

"A Cry for Peace" by Chief Joseph

Tell General Howard I know his heart. What he told me before, I have it in my heart. I am tired of fighting. Our chiefs are killed; Looking-Glass is dead, Ta-Hool-Hool-Shute is dead. The old men are all dead. It is the young men who say yes or no. He who led on the young men is dead. It is cold, and we have no blankets; the little children are freezing to death. My people, some of them, have run away to the hills, and have no blankets, no food. No one knows where they are—perhaps freezing to death. I want to have time to look for my children, and see how many of them I can find. Maybe I shall find them among the dead. Hear me, my chiefs! I am tired; my heart is sick and sad. From where the sun now stands I will fight no more forever.

Readers mark up texts in a lot of different ways. In fact, there is no right way or wrong way to do it. Here are 6 general ways readers respond to texts.

1. Mark or Highlight
With a pen, underline or circle words that are important or seem confusing. With a colorful marker, go over parts of a reading. By marking part of a text, you set off important parts and make these parts easier to find.

2. Question
Form questions as you read. Ask questions such as, "Do I do this?" and ask questions of the author such as, "Is this true?" This is a way of talking with the author. It triggers thoughts in your mind and makes the reading more meaningful.

3. Clarify
"What does this mean?" You probably ask that question as you read. We try to make clear to ourselves what we have read. Often we will write out a thought in our own words—for example, "This means surrender." Other times we might number or label parts of a text to keep track of events in the plot, arguments an author is making, or connections from one page to another.

4. Visualize
When you read, you see mental pictures of what the writer is describing. To help remember these mental pictures, you can also draw what you see. You may make a chart or organizer or draw a picture or sketch. All of these ways of visualizing are useful.

5. Predict
Another common way of responding to literature is to guess what will happen next. "How will this story come out in the end?" Readers make predictions as they read. It is a way of keeping interest in a selection and giving a reason to finish reading a text.

6. React and Connect
Readers often sound off, jotting notes and comments in the margins of books. This, too, is a way of getting more from your reading. It helps you state your own views by noting them and by making a personal connection to what you read.

9

Use these response strategies in the Response Notes space beside each selection in this *Sourcebook*. Look back at these examples whenever you need to.

Now try some of them out. Mark up the text below any way you want. Try to use at least 2 or 3 response strategies.

RESPONSE NOTES

"A Farewell Tribute to Gandhi" by Jawaharlal Nehru

Friends and comrades, the light has gone out of our lives and there is darkness everywhere. I do not know what to tell you and how to say it. Our beloved leader, <u>Bapu</u> as we called him, the father of the nation, is no more. Perhaps I am wrong to say that. Nevertheless, we will not see him again as we have seen him for these many years. We will not run to him for advice and seek <u>solace</u> from him, and that is a terrible blow, not to me only, but to millions and millions in this country, and it is a little difficult to soften the blow by any other advice that I or anyone else can give you.

The light has gone out, I said, and yet I was wrong. For the light that shone in this country was no ordinary light. The light that has <u>illumined</u> this country for these many years will illumine this country for many more years, and a thousand years later that light will still be seen in this country and the world will see it and it will give solace to <u>innumerable</u> hearts. For that light represented the living truth . . . the eternal truths, reminding us of the right path, drawing us from error, taking this ancient country to freedom.

VOCABULARY

Bapu—name for Gandhi, an Indian spiritual leader (1869–1948) who helped to free India from Great Britain through nonviolent protest. Nehru was Gandhi's disciple.
solace—comfort.
illumined—brightened; in this case Gandhi is credited with enlightening India both spiritually and intellectually.
innumerable—countless.

Learning

Making Friends

School Days

School is a time for learning and maturing. It is also a time for making friends and for finding out about oneself.

Searching

Exploring

Readers never begin reading empty-handed. They bring with them all of the ideas, opinions, and experiences they've had. Those experiences help them understand what they read.

BEFORE YOU READ

Read the title of the selection and think about your own school experiences.

1. Consider each statement and put a check mark (√) in the agree/disagree column. Compare answers with a partner.
2. After you finish reading the selection, consider each statement again. Put a check mark (√) in the agree/disagree column.

ANTICIPATION/REACTION GUIDE

BEFORE READING			AFTER READING	
agree	disagree		agree	disagree
☐	☐	1. COMING TO THE UNITED STATES FROM ANOTHER COUNTRY IS ALWAYS DIFFICULT.	☐	☐
☐	☐	2. AN AMERICAN ISLAMIC WOMAN MUST ALWAYS COVER HER HEAD IN PUBLIC.	☐	☐
☐	☐	3. IT'S BETTER TO STAND OUT THAN TO BLEND IN.	☐	☐
☐	☐	4. ALL PEOPLE HAVE A LITTLE BIT OF PREJUDICE IN THEM.	☐	☐
☐	☐	5. STUDENTS CAN BE CRUELEST TO THEIR OWN CLASSMATES.	☐	☐

II. READ

Read the selection from "High School: The Bad and the Good."
1. **Highlight** with a pen or marker the parts that relate to your questions.
2. Write your thoughts in the Response Notes.

"High School: The Bad and the Good"
by Richard Wormser

The <u>rumor</u> had spread around the school since Tuesday. A <u>Muslim</u> girl, no one knew who, had been walking home from school when a car suddenly pulled alongside her. A male student she didn't know jumped out and ripped the scarf off her head, blew his nose in it, threw it back at her, jumped back in the car, and drove off, leaving the poor girl in tears.

The problem was that nobody knew if the story was true. Anam, whose family had come to America from <u>Pakistan</u>, felt that even if it wasn't true, it could have been. The World Trade Center in New York had recently been bombed. People had been killed in the <u>explosion</u> and "Muslim fundamentalists" had been arrested and charged. The air was tense and Anam could sense that when people looked at her, their looks were not friendly. And so she made a major decision:

As a Muslim woman, I am required to cover my hair. We do this to avoid attracting men and engaging in <u>flirtations</u>. It is a way of protecting us. In my parents' country, all women are covered, so none of us stand out.

RESPONSE NOTES

EXAMPLE:
Some students like to spread rumors.

VOCABULARY
rumor—story or statement talked about as news without any proof that it is true.
Muslim—follower of the Islamic religion.
Pakistan—country in Southwest Asia, west of India.
explosion—act of bursting with a loud noise, a blowing up. The World Trade Center is a tall building in New York City that was bombed by people suspected to be Muslim terrorists.
flirtations—paying attention to someone in a romantic way without being serious about it.

RESPONSE NOTES

But in America, being covered makes you stand out. I am a very religious person, but I do not want to draw attention to myself. So I decided not to wear my <u>hejab</u> in public.

Anam's problem is one that is shared by many young Muslim women. While their religion requires them to be covered, they feel they need to make <u>compromises</u> for reasons of personal safety.

STOP AND THINK

Why does Anam stop wearing her hejab in public?

....

....

....

....

Although Muslim students are not usually bothered in school, <u>harassment</u> can suddenly <u>escalate</u> in times of <u>crisis</u>. Several Muslim students in southern high schools were slammed against lockers and walls during the Gulf War. Sadeck, a ninth-grade student in New Jersey, remembers how painful it was for her to go to public school after the World Trade Center bombing. "The kids would call me towel-head," she says, "and threaten to remove my hejab to see if I was bald."

VOCABULARY

hejab—wrap worn across the face and around the head of Muslim women.
compromises—issues in a quarrel or agreement that are settled by each person giving up part of what he or she demands.
harassment—trouble; personal attacks.
escalate—increase or expand rapidly.
crisis—deciding point at which a change must come for better or for worse.

"High School: The Bad and the Good" continued

What world events caused harassment of Muslim students?

In Washington, D.C., two young Muslim women were bumped by a man who deliberately crossed the street to walk into them. In Michigan, a female student tried to pull a hejab off the head of a Muslim student and discovered, to her astonishment, that Muslim women are not necessarily pacifists. "She didn't mess with me anymore after that," the Muslim student recalls, adding, "We are taught to avoid fighting if we can, but if we can't, then we should avoid losing."

Most Muslim students learn to handle the <u>petty annoyances</u> from other students without too much difficulty if the

behavior is childish and not <u>vicious</u>. Muhammad Jihad, a student in Ohio, says that after a bomb exploded on a <u>Pan Am jet over Scotland</u>, killing everyone on board, a fellow student asked him if he was the guy who planted the bomb. "It was a stupid thing to say, and I felt as bad as anybody. In fact, I think I felt a lot worse than most." Another student says that when she first entered high school and wore a hejab, some students

VOCABULARY
petty—small, having little importance or value.
annoyances—feeling of anger, impatience, and the like; small troubles.
vicious—very violent and cruel.
Pan Am jet over Scotland—airplane owned by Pan Am that exploded mysteriously over Scotland in 1988, supposedly the work of Arab terrorists.

RESPONSE NOTES

spread a rumor that she was receiving <u>chemotherapy</u> for cancer and that she covered her head because she had lost all her hair. "It was dumb, but that's the kind of thing you have to put up with if you're a Muslim." Tehani El-Ghussein recalls that she was friendly with a Jewish student who sat behind her in class: "I hadn't covered when I first was in class, so he didn't know I was Muslim. Then, when I decided to cover, he was shocked. He asked me if I was Muslim, and I said yes. 'Aren't we supposed to hate each other?' he said. He was kind of kidding, and we were friendly afterwards, but it was never the same."

STOP AND THINK

How were these Muslims affected by the "kidding" of the other students?

....

....

How do you feel about this kind of "kidding"?

....

....

VOCABULARY

chemotherapy—treatment of a disease such as cancer by chemicals that kill diseased cells.

GATHER YOUR THOUGHTS

A. REFLECT Return to the Anticipation/Reaction Guide on page 12.

1. Read each statement again. Decide whether you agree or disagree.

2. On the lines below, explain how and why your attitudes have changed as a result of reading "High School: The Bad and the Good."

B. DISCUSS Now get together in a small group.

1. Discuss each group member's reaction to the selection.

2. Note your answers to these discussion questions and share them with the class.

DISCUSSION QUESTIONS

HIGH SCHOOL

1. Which is better: to stand out or blend in? Why?

2. Do all people have a little bit of prejudice in them?

3. Why do you think people are threatened by those different from themselves?

TIPS FOR DISCUSSION

☞ Listen carefully.
☞ Be respectful.
☞ Build on each other's ideas.
☞ Disagreement is permitted; argument is not.

IV. WRITE

Write a **paragraph** explaining your answer to one of the discussion questions from the previous page.

1. Start with a topic sentence that clearly answers the question. If possible, draw on specific personal experiences.

2. Use the Writers' Checklist to help you revise.

WRITERS' CHECKLIST

CAPITALIZATION
Did you capitalize:

☐ the first word in a sentence?

☐ proper nouns (the names of particular persons, places, or things)?

EXAMPLES: *Dr. Bedford, Chicago, the Declaration of Independence*

☐ proper adjectives (adjectives formed from proper nouns)?

EXAMPLES: *Asian students, European customs, Japanese diplomat*

☐ the pronoun *I*?

V. WRAP-UP

What, in your own words, was "High School: The Bad and the Good" about?

Do you see pictures in your mind when you read? Do you make mental movies of the characters, setting, and action? This is called visualizing, and it can help you understand and remember what you are reading.

BEFORE YOU READ

Choose a reader to begin. Have the reader read the article's title and opening paragraphs on the next page.

1. Listen carefully. Try to visualize what is being described.

2. Complete the Listener's Guide.

LISTENER'S GUIDE

"FINDING PATRICK"

DIRECTIONS: Answer each question as best you can. If you can't answer a question, leave it blank and come back to the questions later.

WHERE DOES THE ACTION TAKE PLACE?

WHEN DOES THE ACTION TAKE PLACE?

WHO IS PATRICK?

WHAT KIND OF LIFE DOES PATRICK HAVE?

WHAT DO YOU THINK THE TITLE MEANS?

READ

Read the rest of the article with a partner.
1. Take turns reading aloud.
2. As you listen, try to **visualize** what's happening in your mind and sketch what you see in the Response Notes.

"Finding Patrick" by Paul Galloway

RESPONSE NOTES

When a group of tourists from Chicago came to his village in <u>Kenya</u> in the fall of 1993, Patrick Ntutu was at the lowest point in his young life.

He had hoped to be one of the few members of his Masai tribe to go to college, but after completing high school a few months earlier, he learned he had fallen short by a single point on the nationwide examination that determines who can enroll in the country's four universities.

He was devastated.

It seemed he would be spending the rest of his life as a <u>herdsman</u>, tending his father's cattle as they grazed on the tribal grasslands from sunrise to sunset, seven days a week, which was what he had been doing since early childhood, except for the periods when he was permitted to attend school.

It did not matter that he was a son of Lerionka ole Ntutu, a respected Masai chief. It was the duty of all Masai males, whoever their father might be, to care for their families' herds, which are the source of individual wealth and the basis of the tribal economy.

The arrival of the Chicagoans, however, changed everything for the better for Patrick Ntutu.

Thanks to them, he received the money he needed for college, and in August of 1994 he traveled the 35 miles from his rural village to bustling Nairobi, boarded an airplane for the first time and flew to the United States to pursue the dream he thought was lost.

EXAMPLE:

VOCABULARY
Kenya—country in eastern Africa whose capital is Nairobi.
herdsman—person who takes care of a herd, such as of goats, cattle, or sheep.

"It was a <u>miracle</u>," Ntutu said recently, a few days before graduating from Roosevelt University with a degree in business administration. "I never used to believe in miracles. Now I do."

Perhaps it *was* a miracle. Perhaps that is the best explanation for what happened.

The 1993 Chicago tour to Kenya was organized by the Michael Jordan Foundation and led by Deloris Jordan, Michael's mother and the president of his foundation.

Its purpose was to expand the horizons of six 6th graders from the Chicago Public Schools who had won a citywide contest by showing the most improvement in grades, attendance and attitude. Funding was provided by the Chicago Bulls organization and some of the companies whose products Jordan endorses.

"We hadn't planned to bring a Kenyan student back to Chicago," said Deloris Jordan. . . . "Finding Patrick was totally unexpected."

DOUBLE-ENTRY JOURNAL

DIRECTIONS: In the left-hand column are quotes from the article. Read each quotation. Then use the right-hand column to record how it makes you feel.

QUOTES	MY REACTION
"I never used to believe in miracles. Now I do."	
"Finding Patrick was totally unexpected."	

Indeed, she had not wanted to make the trip, for the <u>departure</u> fell only a few weeks after the death of her husband, James, who was shot to death during a robbery in North Carolina.

VOCABULARY
miracle—wonderful happening that is contrary to the laws of nature.
departure—act of going away; leaving.

"Finding Patrick" continued

But the six children had begged her to go, and at the last minute she had agreed.

The itinerary called for a stay of several days in a Masai village, which proved to be Ololulunga, population 1,000, the home of the Ntutu clan.

"We slept in tents in the village compound," Jordan said. "One morning the roar of a lion woke us up, and at night we'd hear a clump-clump-clump. It was *elephants!*"

She smiled. "Our kids were shocked," she said. "They saw that life there was a lot harder than in Chicago. There was no electricity or plumbing. Drinking water was hauled to the village in buckets from a river."

What was most affecting, she said, was the Masai hospitality and the opportunity to meet Lerionka ole Ntutu, the chief, and become acquainted with his wife Natana and their daughter Beatrice.

DOUBLE-ENTRY

JOURNAL

QUOTE	MY REACTION
"One morning the roar of a lion woke us up. . . ."	

"It turned out to be a very emotional experience for me," she said. "At one point, I went off by myself and prayed. I asked God what I could do to help."

Because an emphasis of the Michael Jordan Foundation was education, she decided it would be appropriate to offer a college scholarship to one of the young people in the village. She huddled with the representatives of the sponsoring companies and a Bulls executive who were on the tour, and they pledged to come up with the financing.

The first choice was Beatrice Ntutu, who was in her 20s, but she said her family child-care responsibilities prevented her from accepting. She asked if she could recommend a younger brother, Patrick, who had attended Roman Catholic mission schools, as she had, and who was bright, disciplined, and deserving.

His given name is Keturet (pronounced kay-too-RETT); Patrick is the Christian saint's name he received at baptism.

"I chose St. Patrick because Beatrice told me of a great American basketball player named Patrick Ewing," he said. "Unfortunately, she had not heard of the great Michael Jordan, or I might have been named after St. Michael."

The Chicagoans were impressed with Patrick, who became the only person from outside this country to receive a Michael Jordan Foundation Scholarship. . . .

One of the things that impressed them was his resolve. Indeed, the challenges he faced in getting an education are a rebuke to any of us middle-class Americans who may be compelled now and then to complain about how tough we had it as kids.

DOUBLE-ENTRY JOURNAL

QUOTE	MY REACTION
"Indeed, the challenges he faced in getting an education are a rebuke to any of us middle-class Americans who may be compelled now and then to complain about how tough we had it as kids."	

VOCABULARY
resolve—determination.
rebuke—scolding; expression of disapproval.
compelled—driven to; likely to.

"Finding Patrick" continued

Ntutu lived with his mother and five brothers and sisters in one of the Masais' distinctive one-room dwellings called a manyatta, which is made of mud, tree branches and reeds. (The chief resided in a separate manyatta.)

Every weekday from elementary school through high school, he arose quietly before dawn to move the family's cows from their overnight corral to the milking pen.

By 6 a.m., he returned to the manyatta to change into his school uniform of navy blue shorts and a light blue shirt under a navy blue sweater; he then put on his sandals, grabbed his book bag and set out to run the six miles to school.

Going on foot was necessary because there were no cars, no school buses, and no public transportation; in fact, there were no roads.

Running was necessary because it was the only way to arrive on time for the first class at 8:30 a.m. It took more than two hours to run the six miles because the trail was pocked with large stones and sliced by deep ravines, and his route took him over two mountains.

"This is why Kenya has many good distance runners," he said. "We run because we have to run."

And while traffic and crime were not concerns, wild animals were.

"I can look out from my village and see lions, hyenas, (Cape) buffalo, giraffes, elephants, zebras, monkeys," he said. "That's why we have a fence around our village."

When he was 15, a friend the same age was killed by a lion while watching his family's cattle in a pasture near the village.

VOCABULARY
(Cape) buffalo—large, black horned animals related to cattle but much larger.

"Finding Patrick" continued

When he was 12, he and a friend were returning home from school when they were attacked by a Cape buffalo. "We saw it running at us in time, and we climbed a tree," he said. "It turned dark before he left our tree, and we could start running home again."

DOUBLE-ENTRY JOURNAL

QUOTE	MY REACTION
"Running was necessary because it was the only way to arrive on time for the first class at 8:30 a.m."	

Not surprisingly, he finds Chicago is simpler in some ways.

"Now I live in a <u>dorm</u>, and I take an elevator to my classes," he said. "And I like to run here because it is so flat and smooth. I run on the lakefront early in the morning, and I have run in every Chicago <u>marathon</u> since I've been here."

Some things, of course, have not been so easy.

For one thing, he was unfamiliar with computers. "In Kenya, we hand-write all our studies," he said. "But now I can use the Internet and send e-mail to my family in Kenya" through a government site in Nairobi.

For another thing, classes were conducted differently. "I was used to studying for one national test each year, and here there are many tests. Sometimes, I got tired and wanted to be lazy. Then I said to myself, 'I can't. I must do my best. My family and my tribe are depending on me.'"

At the beginning, there was also a question about his course of study.

"When he got here, he wanted to be a <u>chef</u>," Jordan said, shaking her head.

VOCABULARY

dorm—short for *dormitory*, or a building with many rooms in which to sleep.
marathon—any long foot race, and specifically one of slightly more than 26 miles.
chef—head cook, especially in a restaurant.

"Finding Patrick" continued

"I wanted to study hotel management," he said, smiling.

"I told him if he studied hotel management, I'd put him on the next plane home," she said. "He didn't come to Chicago to learn how to cook."

Ntutu laughed. "I call Mrs. Jordan my second mom," he said. "I am so glad she made me change. Now I want to work in a bank so I can help development in my country. And I also want to start a company of my own."

He has followed his interest in the hospitality industry by working for the last three years at Michael Jordan's Restaurant, 500 N. La Salle St.

"He's a star for us," said Mindy Moore, the restaurant's director of catering and special events. "We started him clearing tables as a houseman, which was hard for him at first because he was so skinny. But he's become one of our top waiters. We serve a lot of school groups, and students love him. He has a great personality and charm and humor, and the patience of a saint. Plus he knows the big guy—Michael."

With the savings from his job, he has paid for a brother to attend one of Kenya's best private schools and a friend to be trained as a teacher, and he has built the first Western-style house in his village.

DOUBLE-ENTRY JOURNAL

QUOTE	MY REACTION
"I must do my best. My family and my tribe are depending on me."	

VOCABULARY
hotel management—career of learning how to run a hotel and restaurant.
development—growth.
hospitality—restaurant and hotel.

The two-bedroom, concrete-block house, which he designed, sits on land that he owns as the son of a Masai chief, and it has become both a tourist attraction and a center of controversy.

"People from <u>Nairobi</u> drive to our village to look at it," he said. "Some people in the village didn't want me to build it. They said it would discourage tourists. It looked too <u>Western</u>.

"The Masai have always resisted <u>Westernization</u>, because they did not like being a British colony for so many years. My father was against the house, but now he wants one. I said, 'Father, go sell your cows.' But in our culture, we cannot sell our cattle. We milk them or slaughter them, but we never sell them. It is not our way."

Ntutu realizes this may not always be so.

"My people are happy now," he said. "But as time goes by, things will change. I am worried about my culture. I worry that one day it may come to an end. I hope not. There are good things about our Masai way of life and good things about the way of life in the West. I hope I can help to keep the good things of our culture."

DOUBLE-ENTRY JOURNAL

QUOTE	MY REACTION
"There are good things about our Masai way of life and good things about the way of life in the West."	

VOCABULARY

Nairobi—capital of Kenya.
Western—of or in the countries of Europe and America.
Westernization—becoming more like the countries of Europe and America.

"Finding Patrick" continued

He was asked if he thinks about being in politics.

He smiled and said, "First, I am trying to find money for an MBA, but when I return home, who knows? Maybe one day, I will be president of my country. That is my goal. I have the skills and the education and the exposure to Western culture to be a good president."

If that happens, this country ought to consider a former NBA player from Chicago named Michael Jordan as our ambassador to Kenya. He ought to have some influence with President Ntutu. Or better yet, how about Jordan's mother?

STOP AND THINK

What is your reaction to Patrick's story?

....

....

....

Which parts of the writing did you find easy to visualize? Why?

....

....

....

VOCABULARY
MBA—Master of Business Administration, which is an advanced business degree.
NBA—National Basketball Association.

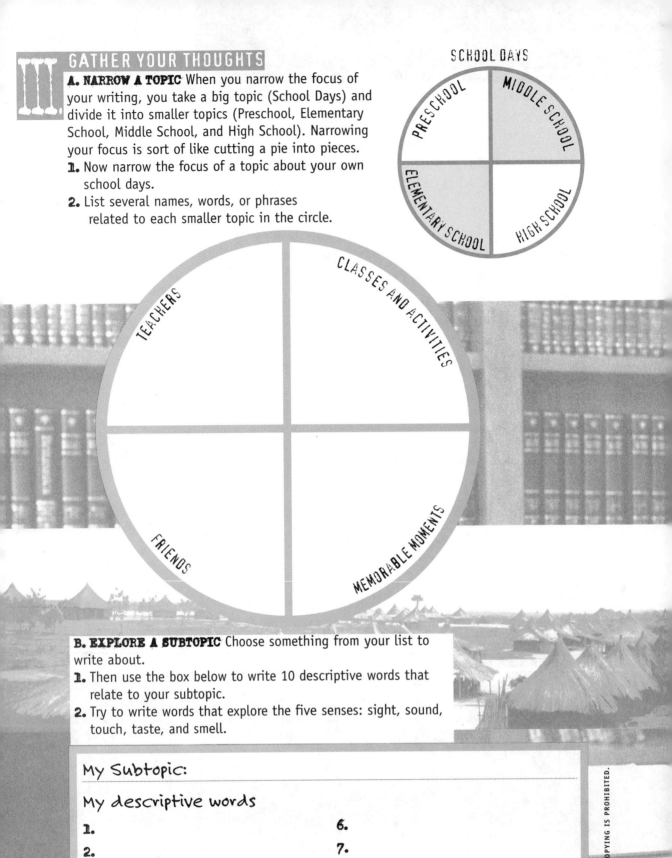

III GATHER YOUR THOUGHTS

A. NARROW A TOPIC When you narrow the focus of your writing, you take a big topic (School Days) and divide it into smaller topics (Preschool, Elementary School, Middle School, and High School). Narrowing your focus is sort of like cutting a pie into pieces.

1. Now narrow the focus of a topic about your own school days.

2. List several names, words, or phrases related to each smaller topic in the circle.

SCHOOL DAYS

PRESCHOOL · MIDDLE SCHOOL · ELEMENTARY SCHOOL · HIGH SCHOOL

TEACHERS · CLASSES AND ACTIVITIES · FRIENDS · MEMORABLE MOMENTS

B. EXPLORE A SUBTOPIC Choose something from your list to write about.

1. Then use the box below to write 10 descriptive words that relate to your subtopic.

2. Try to write words that explore the five senses: sight, sound, touch, taste, and smell.

My Subtopic: ....

My descriptive words

1.   6.

2.   7.

3.   8.

4.   9.

5.   10.

IV. WRITE

Write a **descriptive paragraph** about a subtopic of your School Days.

1. Use your notes on the previous page to help you include as many sensory words as you can.

2. Use the Writers' Checklist to help you revise.

WRITERS' CHECKLIST

PUNCTUATION

Every sentence needs to express a complete thought and should end with a punctuation mark.

❑ Did you use periods correctly? Most sentences end with a period.
EXAMPLE: *The first year was terrible.*

❑ Did you use exclamation marks correctly? Sentences that are meant to be said forcefully end with exclamation marks.
EXAMPLE: *I was terrified!*

❑ Did you use question marks correctly? A question ends with a question mark.
EXAMPLE: *Who is in charge here?*

What impression did the story about Patrick make on you?

READERS'
CHECKLIST

MEANING
☐ Did you learn something from the reading?
☐ Did it affect you or make an impression?

_____

_____

_____

_____

_____

_____

_____

_____

_____

_____

Apartheid

Apartheid means "separateness" in Afrikaans, one of South Africa's official languages. It refers to the period between 1948 and 1991, when South Africa's white-controlled government separated blacks, Asians, and other people of color from the white population. There was segregation in housing, education, jobs, and even transportation.

Nelson Mandela

SOUTH AFRICA

Often you hear, "Get ready." The band conductor, soccer coach, starter at a track meet—all of them say, "Get ready." The same advice is useful for reading.

BEFORE YOU READ

One way to "get ready" to read a story is to think about its subject. "It's Quiet Now" describes life under apartheid.

1. Think about what words or images come to mind when you hear the word *apartheid*.

2. On the arms of the web, write words that capture what you know about *apartheid*.

WORD WEB

APARTHEID

3. Share your web with others in the class. Discuss similarities and differences among the words.

READ

Read the story.

1. As you read, circle the main things that happen. **Clarify** what's happening by jotting comments in the Response Notes.

2. Then fill out the Story Map at the end of the selection.

"It's Quiet Now" by Gcina Mhlope

veryone seems to be going to bed now. The rain is coming down in a steady downpour, and I don't think it's going to stop for a long time. Normally I would be joining the others, going to bed while it's still raining so that I can enjoy the sound of it white I wait for sleep to come and take me. I don't want to play any soft music either. I just want to stand here at the window and watch what can be seen of the rain coming down in the dark.

The news in the papers is always the same—some people's house <u>petrol-bombed</u>, youths and <u>activists</u> arrested, suspected informer <u>necklaced</u>, police shootings—it only varies from place to place. It's been like this for . . . I don't know how long.

It's really depressing. Today I did not even have to buy a paper, things just kept happening since late this morning.

The <u>PUTCO</u> buses have not been going into the <u>townships</u>. Last week they started coming into our township again. The newspapers said that the local Residents' Association had gone to ask the authorities to bring back the buses, but members of the Association know nothing about it. Most old people seemed quite relieved that the buses were back, but they knew it wouldn't last. Company delivery vans have not been coming in either; the students have burnt so many of them in the past few months.

RESPONSE NOTES

EXAMPLE:
Buses coming back despite continuing violence.

VOCABULARY

petrol-bombed—had fire bombs thrown at them.
activists—persons who take or favor direct action to solve political problems.
necklaced—tortured by putting a tire around the neck and setting the tire afire.
PUTCO—name of a large company in South Africa.
townships—areas where blacks lived.

The house of the local "Mayor" was also burnt down. It was at one o'clock after midnight when we were woken up by two loud explosions one after the other, and soon the house was eaten up by hungry flames. The "Mayor" and his family just made it out of the house, running for their lives. Everything was burnt to ashes by the time the police and fire engines arrived. When I saw his house like that, I remembered what he had said a few weeks back in a Residents' meeting.

"You seem to forget that I am as black as you are, and I suffer just like you do under the apartheid laws of this country." The grumbling from the audience showed that nobody believed him.

A lot of things have been happening here; I just can't keep track. Young children who hardly understand what is really going on are also shouting the slogan "Siyayinyova," which simply means, "We will destroy or disrupt."

Nobody was expecting anything today, even though there were more policemen than usual—there have been police driving up and down our streets for quite a while now. We carry on with our work and sort of pretend they are not there.

I was carrying on with my work as well, when I suddenly heard singing. I ran to the window and there, at a school in Eighth Avenue, these children—you know I can still see them as if there's a photograph in my mind. . . . They poured out of their classes into the streets, where the police were. They were shouting "Siyayinyova!" at the tops of their little voices. They picked up rocks and bricks and started attacking buses, company delivery vans and police cars. When the police started chasing them, they ran through double-ups (small paths cutting through people's houses). I stood

VOCABULARY
slogan—motto.
disrupt—break up or cause disorder in.

"It's Quiet Now" CONTINUED

transfixed at the window. There was running everywhere, just school uniforms all over the township, and shouting and chanting and screaming and burning of policemen's and <u>councillors</u>' houses.

Two company vans were burnt in front of the house right opposite us. The fire jumped and caught on to the house as well, and then there was black smoke from the house and the cars in the next street and the next. . . . Soon the streets were lost in the dust and smoke.

Clouds from earth began to meet clouds from the sky. We suddenly heard—ghwara! ghwara! Lightning and thunder! Louder than any bomb or gun. Poor soldiers, their guns came down as the rain began to fall—whhhaaaaa. . . . Maybe it came to clean up the mess.

People started coming back from work. It kept on raining and no one even ran. They walked in the rain as if everything was as they had left it. Some had heard the news from work, and others could see that a lot had happened. But they walked home as usual and got on with their suppers. I didn't have an appetite at supper. I wonder if I should go to sleep now. There is only a light drizzle coming down and all seems quiet in the night.

VOCABULARY

councillors—persons elected by citizens to make laws and manage a city or town.

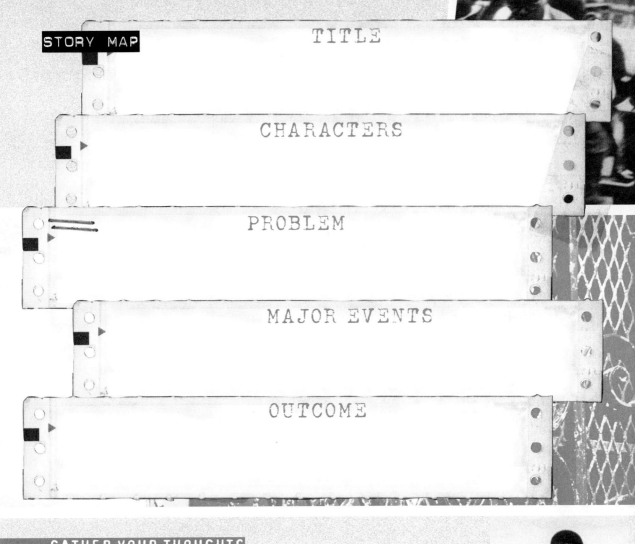

STORY MAP

TITLE

CHARACTERS

PROBLEM

MAJOR EVENTS

OUTCOME

GATHER YOUR THOUGHTS

RESPOND TO A SELECTION Explore your thoughts about the story by writing in a journal.

1. Read each of these "sentence starters."

2. List several ideas after each of the sentence starters.

1. When I was reading, I thought about . . .

2. I noticed that . . .

IV. WRITE

Write a **journal entry** based on your reactions to "It's Quiet Now."
1. Choose one of the sentence starters from the previous page.
   Write it on the first line of your journal entry.
2. Use the Writers' Checklist to help you revise.

WRITERS' CHECKLIST

ARTICLES

Make your writing easy to
understand by using articles (*an,*
a, and *the*) correctly.
- ❑ Did you use *an* before a vowel
  or a vowel sound? EXAMPLE: *It*
  took more than an *hour to fall*
  asleep.
- ❑ Did you use *a* before a
  consonant sound? EXAMPLE:
  Hearing a *bomb scared me.*
- ❑ Did you avoid using *the* with
  nouns that mean *all* or *in*
  general? EXAMPLE: *In Africa*
  apartheid (not the *apartheid)*
  causes much suffering.

V. WRAP-UP

What parts of this story were most enjoyable? Tell what you liked best about what you read.

4 : Survival

Imagine that you were going to the grocery store to buy one item: a brand of cereal. Would you walk down each aisle in the store? Or, would you look just in the cereal aisle?

Just as smart shoppers "skim" through the grocery store, good readers skim to find the answers to questions. They look only for key words and phrases to answer questions. Skimming before you read helps you get a better idea of what to expect.

I. BEFORE YOU READ

Ask yourself a simple question about the selection: "Who and what is "Survival" about?"

1. Next, skim through the selection. Instead of reading every word, look for key words and phrases that help you answer that question.
2. As you skim, trace your finger along the lines of the text very quickly. Look for names, words that are repeated, and phrases in the first and last sentences of each paragraph.
3. Write several of the key words and phrases you find in the boxes below. Use those words to help you answer the question below about "Survival."

SKIM FOR KEY WORDS AND PHRASES

names

repeated words

phrases from beginning and end of each paragraph

Who and what is "Survival" about?

II. READ

Take turns reading the selection aloud.
1. As your partner reads, follow along in the text.
2. Underline any words or ideas that are difficult or unfamiliar to you.
3. Write a **question** in the Response Notes near any parts that you don't understand or that you want to discuss.

RESPONSE NOTES

EXAMPLE:
Who did she ask for money?

"Survival" from *Kaffir Boy* by Mark Mathabane

To prevent us from starving and to maintain a roof over our heads, my mother began running around the township soliciting money with which to pay the rent and to buy food, but very little came of it. A few people tried to help; but in the main, black people were burdened with their own survival.

When it seemed that no help was forthcoming, we resigned ourselves to the inevitable: eviction and starvation. Luck of some sort came when my maternal grandmother—who had been away in the Shangaan Bantustan attending a ceremony to exorcise evil spirits from a raving mad relative—came back unexpectedly. My mother told her of our plight. Granny had some money to spare.

VOCABULARY
soliciting—asking earnestly and sincerely for; requesting; trying to get.
burdened—weighed down; thinking almost completely about.
resigned—submitted quietly to; yielded.
inevitable—sure to happen.
eviction—removal from a home.
exorcise—drive out with prayers.
plight—bad situation.

"Survival" CONTINUED

She paid the rent a week before we were to be evicted; bought us bread, sugar and mealie meal; and gave my mother one hundred cents to take George and Florah to the clinic, where their sickness was diagnosed as advanced malnutrition and chicken pox. More money was required to continue their treatment, and Granny gave my mother three hundred cents. Thinking her rich, I proposed to my mother that we move in with her until my father's return from prison. My mother told me that that could not be, that Granny was already overburdened with looking after herself and her other children and could not afford to take us in. Moreover, my mother said, my father's relatives would never sanction such a move.

"Why?" I asked. "We're starving as it is, and they aren't helping us in any way." I had close to a dozen relatives on my father's side scattered all over Johannesburg; yet since my father's arrest none had come forward to help us.

stop and clarify

What is the plight, or situation, of this family?

My mother explained that my father's relatives would not allow us to move in with any of her relatives because according to tribal marriage customs we were my father's property—her, myself, my brother and my sister; therefore, for as long as my father was alive, regardless of his being in prison, we had to stay put in his kaya (house), awaiting his eventual return.

VOCABULARY

mealie meal—food similar to corn meal.
diagnosed—found out through examination or tests.
malnutrition—poorly nourished or underfed.
chicken pox—disease of children that causes a rash on the skin.
sanction—allow.
Johannesburg—major city in northeastern South Africa.
tribal marriage customs—habits of the tribe when two people become husband and wife.

©GREAT SOURCE. COPYING IS PROHIBITED.

RESPONSE NOTES

The money Granny gave us soon ran out. Granny could no longer help us because what she had given us had been her "last money." My father was still not back. Where would we get rent money? Food money?

There was a small grocery store nearby where my father, before his arrest, had maintained a simple charge account. It worked in the following way: during the week he would buy things like candies, tea, sugar, paraffin, bread, matches, mealie meal and floor polish, on credit; and on Friday, payday for him, he would settle the account. But since his arrest, the account had not been used. One afternoon my mother and I went to the store to see if we could reopen it. The storekeeper, a lean Mosotho man with greying hair, told us we could not reopen the account, for there was no man in our house to settle it on Fridays. As my mother and I turned to leave, the storekeeper called us back. There was a way he could try and help us. If my mother would work at cleaning his house and washing his family's clothing, he could arrange to pay our rent. My mother agreed. She would be required to work on weekends. So our rent problem was taken care of. Now what about food? Word

STOP AND PREDICT

Where do you think the family will find food?

_____

_____

_____

came that a new garbage dump, the Mlothi, had just opened, and many of Alexandra's poor were going there in search of scraps of food. We decided to go there too.

"I never thought the day would come when we would have to do this," my mother said.

■ VOCABULARY ■
paraffin—white, wax-like material used for sealing jars or making candles.
Alexandra's—of the town of Alexandra, in South Africa.

"Survival" CONTINUED

The Mlothi was on the veld fringing Alexandra to the coast, about half a mile from where we lived. Every weekday huge, grey trucks arrived to dump garbage from white people's homes. Each morning my mother would take Florah, George and me, and the four of us would join the throng of black men, women and children flocking down there. We always left home between six and seven in the morning so we could be among the front wave of people rushing the trucks as they came in, usually around ten.

The Mlothi provided us with many items we could not afford—clothes, knives, furniture, spoons, cribs, mugs, forks, plates and scraps of food. All at no cost. We simply had to be there very early in the morning, wait for the trucks to arrive and dump and then carefully dig our way through the heap of ash and refuse, collecting item after item as we worked the huge mound till sundown.

We would use sticks and iron rods to dig, but often we had to use our hands, especially on Mondays and Tuesdays when the garbage contained perishables like half-eaten sandwiches and cold cuts. One morning I was digging alongside my sister when my stick struck something soft buried deep in the debris.

"Mama!" I cried, "I think I've found something nice."

My mother, digging a couple yards away from me, asked what it was I had found.

stop and clarify

How would you describe what being poor means? Does this family seem poor?

....

....

VOCABULARY

veld—open country of South Africa, with grass and bushes but few trees.
fringing—bordering or running along the outside of.
throng—large crowd.
refuse—garbage, waste, useless stuff or junk.
perishables—things that will likely spoil or decay, especially food.
debris—rubbish; scattered fragments of junk.

"I don't know yet," I said. "But it felt soft. It must be food. And it's big."

Upon hearing the word *food*, all the ashen-faced men, women and children digging about me started inching toward where I was digging, their faces lit with expectation. "Mama!" I yelled, remembering previous fights which had erupted when families fought over rights to dig up white people's <u>leftovers</u>.

"Don't dig in my child's territory!" my mother screamed a warning and hurried over to protect my discovery by staking out the area I was digging in.

?? STOP aND QueSTiON ??

What are some of the health problems of digging for food in a garbage dump?

_____

_____

_____

"Where's your find, child?" she asked, sliding over to me.

"In there," I pointed excitedly at the huge mound where I was digging. "Among the broken bottles and papers."

My mother began digging delicately around the area, first with her stick, to clear the broken bottles, then with her <u>gnarled</u> hands to reach the object. My sister and I joined her in the digging. My brother was strapped to my mother's back.

"Careful about using your hands," she warned. "There's too much broken glass."

VOCABULARY
leftovers—scraps.
gnarled—rough and twisted.

"Survival" CONTINUED

My sister and I stopped digging, and we waited expectantly alongside, our mouths drooling. One of the women digging nearby said to my mother, enviously:

"Musadi [woman], your children are lucky. They are the best diggers around. They seem to always know where the good things are. Just look at those sacks and boxes you have there with you; they're already full, and it isn't noon yet. I wish my children were like that, instead of the lazy fools my husband gave me." At that, she turned and pinched the ear of one of her children, a boy my age, and said, "Come on, dig! Why aren't you like Johannes! He finds his mother things, and you don't find me anything! You just eat, eat, eat!"

VOCABULARY
expectantly—thinking as if something is likely to happen.
drooling—dripping saliva.

[stop and summarize]

What were the two main problems the Mathabane family members faced?

_____

_____

_____

_____

GATHER YOUR THOUGHTS

A. RECOGNIZE IMPORTANT INFORMATION What did this selection make you think about? What did it teach you about life under apartheid for black Africans?

1. Look over the list of key words and phrases you wrote on page 34. Use them to help you think about what "Survival" is about.

2. Complete the following sentence:

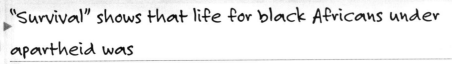

"Survival" shows that life for black Africans under

apartheid was

1. _____ and

2. _____ .

B. PLAN Get ready to write a letter that describes 2 things about life under apartheid. Use the organizer below to plan the body of your letter.

1. Decide which topic should go first and which second. Save the more important point for last.

2. Reread "Survival," looking for details about each of your topics. List 2 or more details in each box.

TOPIC 1	TOPIC 2

IV. WRITE

Imagine a friend has asked you, "What was it like for black Africans living under apartheid?" Write a **letter** to answer that question.

1. Organize the letter around your description of 2 aspects of living under apartheid.

2. Use the Writers' Checklist to help you revise.

WRITERS' CHECKLIST

COMMAS

❑ **Did you place a comma at the end of the greeting of your friendly letter?** EXAMPLES: *Dear Andy, Dear Ms. Dunn,*

❑ **Did you place a comma after the day in the date?** EXAMPLE: *January 7, 2000*

❑ **Did you place a comma after the closing of your friendly letter?** EXAMPLES: *Yours truly, Sincerely,*

V. WRAP-UP

What made "Survival" easy or difficult to read?

Zora Neale Hurston

Zora Neale Hurston

Zora Neale Hurston (1891–1960) was born in the all-black town of Eatonville, Florida. After college, she moved to New York City, where she gained instant fame as a writer and became known for wearing outrageous clothing and big hats. Hurston's writing celebrates African-American culture.

ZORA NEALE HURSTON

Edited and with an introduction by Robert E. Hemenway

Dust Tracks on a Road
An Autobiography
Second Edition · Including Previously Unpublished Chapters

5: How It Feels to Be Colored Me

What's your story? In a personal narrative, the writer shares a story from his or her own life. Knowing an author's purpose helps you to know what to read for.

BEFORE YOU READ

Consider this question: "What's Zora Neale Hurston's story?" Take a minute to preview the narrative she wrote.

1. Spend 1 minute glancing through the selection. ....

2. Make some notes on the chart below.

Preview Chart

Answer each question. Your answer may or may not be right. That doesn't matter. What matters is that you have begun to think about Zora Neale Hurston before you begin reading.

WHAT'S ZORA NEALE HURSTON'S STORY?

Who's involved?

What's happening?

When and where does it take place?

READ

Read "How It Feels to Be Colored Me" at your own pace.

1. Put a check-mark (√) in the margin when you learn something interesting about Zora Neale Hurston.

2. If you come across a word you don't know, **highlight** it. Use the Response Notes to make a guess about its possible meaning.

Response Notes

"How It Feels to Be Colored Me" from *I Love Myself When I'm Laughing* by Zora Neale Hurston

I am colored but I offer nothing in the way of extenuating circumstances except the fact that I am the only Negro in the United States whose grandfather on the mother's side was *not* an Indian chief.

I remember the very day that I became colored. Up to my thirteenth year I lived in the little Negro town of Eatonville, Florida. It is exclusively a colored town. The only white people I knew passed through the town going to or coming from Orlando. The native whites rode dusty horses, the Northern tourists chugged down the sandy village road in automobiles. The town knew the Southerners and never stopped cane chewing when they passed. But the Northerners were something else again. They were peered at cautiously from behind curtains by the timid. The more venturesome would come out on the porch to watch them go past and got just as much pleasure out of the tourists as the tourists got out of the village.

The front porch might seem a daring place for the rest of the town, but it was a gallery seat for me. My favorite place was atop the gate-post. Proscenium box for a born first-nighter. Not only did I enjoy the show, but I didn't mind the actors knowing that I liked it. I

EXAMPLE:
Is it like chewing gum?

VOCABULARY

extenuating circumstances—excuses.
exclusively—not shared with others.
timid—easily frightened; shy.
venturesome—risky; adventurous.
Proscenium box—platform or stage for speaking.

F.M.CLARK
MILESTON STORE.

usually spoke to them in passing. I'd wave at them and when they returned my <u>salute</u>, I would say something like this: "Howdy-do-well-I-thank-you-where-you-goin'?" Usually automobile or the horse paused at this, and after a queer exchange of <u>compliments</u>, I would probably "go a piece of the way" with them, as we say in farthest Florida. If one of my family happened to come to the front in time to see me, of course <u>negotiations</u> would be rudely broken off. But even so, it is clear that I was the first "welcome-to-our-state" Floridian, and I hope the Miami Chamber of Commerce will please take notice.

stop + think

In your own words, what did Hurston like about being on the front porch?

....

....

....

stop + think

During this period, white people differed from colored to me only in that they rode through town and never lived there. They liked to hear me "speak pieces" and sing and wanted to see me dance the <u>parse-me-la</u>, and gave me generously of their small silver for doing these things, which seemed strange to me for I wanted to do them so much that I needed bribing to stop. Only they didn't know it. The colored people gave no dimes. They <u>deplored</u> any joyful <u>tendencies</u> in me, but I was their Zora nevertheless. I belonged to them, to the nearby hotels, to the county—everybody's Zora.

VOCABULARY

salute—greeting with a polite gesture.
compliments—expressions of praise or admiration.
negotiations—talks or discussions leading to agreements with other people.
parse-me-la—kind of dance.
deplored—disapproved of.
tendencies—habits; inclinations to think, act, or behave in a certain way.

"How It Feels to Be Colored Me" continued

But changes came in the family when I was thirteen, and I was sent to school in Jacksonville. I left Eatonville, the town of the <u>oleanders</u>, as Zora. When I disembarked from the riverboat at Jacksonville, she was no more. It seemed that I had suffered a sea change. I was not Zora of Orange County anymore, I was now a little colored girl. I found it out in certain ways. In my heart as well as in the mirror, I became a fast brown—warranted not to rub nor run.

But I am not tragically colored. There is no great sorrow dammed up in my soul, nor lurking behind my eyes. I do not mind at all. I do not belong to the sobbing school of Negrohood who hold that nature somehow has given them a lowdown dirty deal and whose feelings are all hurt about it. Even in the helter-skelter skirmish that is my life, I have seen that the world is to the strong regardless of a little <u>pigmentation</u> more or less. No, I do not weep at the world—I am too busy <u>sharpening my oyster knife</u>.

stop+think

How did Hurston's feelings about herself change once she moved to Jacksonville?

....

....

....

....

stop+think

VOCABULARY
oleanders—flowering plants.
pigmentation—coloring.
sharpening my oyster knife—Hurston probably uses this expression to mean that she is too busy studying, exploring, and learning about the world. An oyster knife is used for prying open the shell of an oyster to find what's inside.

"How It Feels to Be Colored Me" continued

Someone is always at my elbow reminding me that I am the granddaughter of slaves. It fails to register depression with me. Slavery is sixty years in the past. The operation was successful and the patient is doing well, thank you. The terrible struggle that made me an American out of a potential slave said "On the line!" The Reconstruction said "Get set!"; and the generation before said "Go!" I am off to a flying start and I must not halt in the stretch to look behind and weep. Slavery is the price I paid for <u>civilization</u>, and the choice was not with me. It is a bully adventure and worth all that I have paid through my ancestors for it. No one on earth ever had a greater chance for glory. The world to be won and nothing to be lost. It is thrilling to think—to know that for any act of mine, I shall get twice as much praise or twice as much blame. It is quite exciting to hold the center of the national stage, with the spectators not knowing whether to laugh or to weep.

stop + think

How have Hurston's ancestors helped her?

....

....

....

stop + think

The position of my white neighbor is much more difficult. No brown <u>specter</u> pulls up a chair beside me when I sit down to eat. No dark ghost thrusts its leg against mine in bed. The game of keeping what one has is never so exciting as the game of getting.

VOCABULARY

civilization—Hurston here uses a metaphor, "Slavery is the price I paid for civilization." She explains that she enjoys a life with a high level of development—good education, culture, and comfort—because of the terrible price paid by her ancestors who were slaves.
specter—phantom.

"How It Feels to Be Colored Me" continued

I do not always feel colored. Even now I often achieve the unconscious Zora of Eatonville before the <u>Hegira</u>. I feel most colored when I am thrown against a sharp white background. For instance at <u>Barnard</u>. "Beside the waters of the Hudson" I feel my race. Among the thousand white persons, I am a dark rock surged upon, and overswept, but through it all, I remain myself. When covered by the waters, I am; and the ebb but reveals me again.

stop+think

Describe in your own words how Hurston feels at Barnard.

....

....

....

stop+think

Sometimes it is the other way around. A white person is set down in our midst, but the contrast is just as sharp for me. For instance, when I sit in the drafty basement that is The New World Cabaret with a white person, my color comes. We enter chatting about any little nothing that we have in common and are seated by the jazz waiters. In the abrupt way that jazz orchestras have, this one plunges into a number. It loses no time in <u>circumlocutions</u>, but gets right down to business. It constricts the <u>thorax</u> and splits the heart with its tempo and <u>narcotic harmonies</u>. This orchestra grows <u>rambunctious</u>, rears on its hind legs and attacks the tonal veil with primitive fury, rending it, clawing it until it breaks through to the jungle beyond. I follow those heathen—follow them exultingly. I dance wildly inside myself; I yell within, I whoop; I shake my

■ VOCABULARY ■
Hegira—historical reference to Mohammed's flight to Mecca, the Muslim Holy Land.
Barnard—college in New York.
circumlocutions—wordy language that does not get to the point.
thorax—part of the human body between the neck and the diaphragm (about halfway down the chest).
narcotic harmonies—soothing or numbing sounds.
rambunctious—loud and disorderly.

assegai above my head, I hurl it true to the mark
yeeeeooww! I am in the jungle and living in the jungle
way. My face is painted red and yellow and my body is
painted blue. My pulse is throbbing like a war drum. I
want to slaughter something—give pain, give death to
what, I do not know. But the piece ends. The men of the
orchestra wipe their lips and rest their fingers. I creep
back slowly to the veneer we call civilization with the
last tone and find the white friend sitting motionless in
his seat, smoking calmly.

"Good music they have here," he remarks,
drumming the table with his fingertips.

Music. The great blobs of purple and red emotion
have not touched him. He has only heard what I felt.
He is far away and I see him but dimly across the
ocean and the continent that have fallen between us.
He is so pale with his whiteness then and I am so
colored.

stop+think

Why do you think Hurston tells the story about the jazz club?

....

....

....

....

stop+think

At certain times I have no race, I am *me*. When I set
my hat at a certain angle and saunter down Seventh
Avenue, Harlem City, feeling as snooty as the lions in
front of the Forty-Second Street Library, for instance. So
far as my feelings are concerned, Peggy Hopkins Joyce

VOCABULARY
assegai—light spear or lance.
veneer—superficial surface or base.
saunter—stroll or walk.
snooty—snobbish; feeling superior or above another person.

"How It Feels to Be Colored Me" continued

on the Boule Mich with her gorgeous raiment, stately carriage, knees knocking together in a most aristocratic manner, has nothing on me. The cosmic Zora emerges. I belong to no race nor time. I am the eternal feminine with its string of beads.

I have no separate feeling about being an American citizen and colored. I am merely a fragment of the Great Soul that surges within the boundaries. My country, right or wrong.

Sometimes, I feel discriminated against, but it does not make me angry. It merely astonishes me. How can any deny themselves the pleasure of my company? It's beyond me.

But in the main, I feel like a brown bag of miscellany propped against a wall. Against a wall in company with other bags, white, red, and yellow. Pour out the contents, and there is discovered a jumble of small things priceless and worthless. A first-water diamond, an empty spool, bits of broken glass, lengths of string, a key to a door long since crumbled away, a rusty knife blade, old shoes saved for a road that never was and never will be, a nail bent under the weight of things too heavy for any nail, a dried flower or two still a little fragrant. In your hand is the brown bag. On the ground before you is the jumble it held—so much like the jumble in the bags, could they be emptied, that all might be dumped in a single heap and the bags refilled without altering the content of any greatly. A bit of colored glass more or less would not matter. Perhaps that is how the Great Stuffer of Bags filled them in the first place—who knows?

VOCABULARY
raiment—clothing.
carriage—vehicle that has wheels and carries passengers.
aristocratic—high class; noble.
cosmic—relating to the universe; the unreachable.
emerges—comes into view; appears.
miscellany—various things.

WORD STUDY

UNFAMILIAR WORD	CONTEXT CLUES
EXAMPLE:	
1. parse-me-la	It's a type of dance that can be performed outside; Zora dances it by herself.
2.	
3.	
4.	

GATHER YOUR THOUGHTS

A. MODEL Zora Neale Hurston writes about how her move to Jacksonville caused her to change how she felt about herself.

1. Use 1 of Hurston's sentences as a model to help you plan a personal narrative paragraph.

2. Think of at least 3 ways to complete this sentence.

I remember the very day that . . .

a. _____

b. _____

c. _____

B. DEVELOP THE PARAGRAPH Choose 1 of the topics above as your focus. Organize your own narrative into 3 parts:

1. Topic Sentence Complete the sentence below.

MY TOPIC SENTENCE

What I tell people about my life is . . .

_____

2. Body Write 3 details about your experience that you'll want to tell readers.

Detail #1 _____

Detail #2 _____

Detail #3 _____

3. Closing Sentence Write a closing sentence that sums up why the experience was important to you.

_____

_____

IV. WRITE

Use Hurston's writing as a model to write a **personal narrative** about an experience.

1. Use the topic sentence and details you developed on the previous page.
2. Use the Writers' Checklist to help you revise.

Title:

V. WRAP-UP

What did you find yourself thinking about after reading this selection?

....

....

....

....

....

....

....

....

....

Do you like to tell stories? As a little girl growing up in Eatonville, Florida, Zora Neale Hurston loved to listen to people talk. These stories about what was happening in her town had a strong effect on her writing. Hurston even made her characters' dialogue sound like "the folks at home."

BEFORE YOU READ

Think of the most interesting or unusual person you know.

1. Write 5 or more words describing this person in the spaces below.
2. Get together in a small group. Tell about your person and share your word boxes.
3. Help each other come up with additional descriptions.

Word Box

PERSON I'M DESCRIBING:

II. READ

Read a few stories from "The Eatonville Anthology."
1. As you read, **react** to and make notes about the characters in the Response Notes.
2. Think about which character seems the most interesting and why.

"The Eatonville Anthology" by Zora Neale Hurston

THE PLEADING WOMAN

Mrs. Tony Roberts is the pleading woman. She just loves to ask for things. Her husband gives her all he can rake and scrape, which is considerably more than most wives get for their housekeeping, but she goes from door to door begging for things.

She starts at the store. "Mist' Clarke," she sing-songs in a high keening voice, "gimme lil' piece uh meat tuh boil a pot uh greens wid. Lawd knows me an' mah chillen is SO hongry! Hits uh SHAME! Tony don't fee-ee-eee-ed me!"

Mr. Clarke knows that she has money and that her larder is well stocked, for Tony Roberts is the best provider on his list. But her keening annoys him and he arises heavily. The pleader at this shows all the joy of a starving man being seated at a feast.

"Thass right Mist' Clarke. De Lawd loveth de cheerful giver. Gimme jes' a lil' piece 'bout dis big (indicating the width of her hand) an' de Lawd'll bless yuh. "

She follows this angel-on-earth to his meat tub and superintends the cutting, crying out in pain when he refuses to move the knife over just a teeny bit mo'.

EXAMPLE:
Mrs. Roberts=
greedy?
no pride?

VOCABULARY

keening—loud crying.
gimme lil'—give me a little. Hurston is writing dialect.
mah chillen—my children.
hongry—hungry.
jes'—just.
superintends—looks over; directs.
teeny bit mo'—little bit more.

F.M.CLARK
MILESTON STORE.

Finally, meat in hand, she departs, remarking on the meanness of some people who give a piece of salt meat only two-fingers wide when they were plainly asked for a hand-wide piece. Clarke puts it down to Tony's account and resumes his reading.

stop+think

What words would you use to describe Mrs. Roberts?

....

....

stop+think

With the slab of salt pork as a foundation, she visits various homes until she has collected all she wants for the day. At the Piersons, for instance: "Sister Pierson, plee-ee-ease gimme uh han'ful uh collard greens fuh me an' mah po' chillen! 'Deed, me an' mah chillen is SO hongry. Tony doan' fee-ee-eed me!"

Mrs. Pierson picks a bunch of greens for her, but she springs away from them as if they were poison. "Lawd a mussy, Mis' Pierson, you ain't gonna gimme dat lil' eye-full uh greens fuh me an' mah chillen, is you? Don't be so graspin'; Gawd won't bless yuh. Gimme uh han'full mo'. Lawd, some folks is got everything, an' theys jes' as gripin' an stingy!"

Mrs. Pierson raises the ante, and the pleading woman moves on to the next place, and on and on. The next day, it commences all over.

VOCABULARY
slab—flat, thick piece.
foundation—basis on which something rests.
collard greens—dark green vegetables.
mussy—mercy.
ante—price to be paid.
commences—starts.

stop+think

Why do you think Hurston tells the story of Mrs. Tony Roberts?

....

....

stop+think

"The Eatonville Anthology" continued

TURPENTINE LOVE

Jim Merchant is always in good humor—even with his wife. He says he fell in love with her at first sight. That was some years ago. She has had all her teeth pulled out, but they still get along splendidly.

He says the first time he called on her he found out that she was subject to fits. This didn't cool his love, however. She had several in his presence.

One Sunday, while he was there, she had one, and her mother tried to give her a <u>dose</u> of <u>turpentine</u> to stop it. Accidentally, she spilled it in her eye and it cured her. She never had another fit, so they got married and have kept each other in good humor ever since.

VOCABULARY
dose—amount given or taken at one time.
turpentine—oil drawn from the wood of certain pine trees.

stop+think

What is funny or unusual about the story "Turpentine Love"?

....

....

stop+think

THE WAY OF A MAN WITH A TRAIN

Old Man Anderson lived seven or eight miles out in the
country from Eatonville. Over by Lake Apopka. He
raised feed-corn and <u>cassava</u> and went to market with
it two or three times a year. He bought all of his
<u>victuals</u> wholesale so he wouldn't have to come to
town for several months more.

He was different from us <u>citybred </u>folks. He had
never seen a train. Everybody laughed at him for even
the smallest child in Eatonville had either been to
<u>Maitland or Orlando</u> and watched a train go by. On
Sunday afternoons all of the young people of the
village would go over to Maitland, a mile away, to see
Number 35 whizz southward on its way to Tampa and
wave at the passengers. So we looked down on him a
little. Even we children felt superior in the presence of
a person so lacking in worldly knowledge.

The grown-ups kept telling him he ought to go see
a train. He always said he didn't have time to wait so
long. Only two trains a day passed through Maitland.

VOCABULARY
cassava—a kind of bush or shrub.
victuals—food.
citybred—raised in the city.
Maitland or Orlando—cities in central Florida.

"The Eatonville Anthology" continued

But patronage and ridicule finally had its effect and Old Man Anderson drove in one morning early. Number 78 went north to Jacksonville at 10:20. He drove his light wagon over in the woods beside the railroad below Maitland, and sat down to wait. He began to fear that his horse would get frightened and run away with the wagon. So he took him out and led him deeper into the grove and tied him securely. Then he returned to his wagon and waited some more. Then he remembered that some of the train-wise villagers had said the engine belched fire and smoke. He had better move his wagon out of danger. It might catch afire. He climbed down from the seat and placed himself between the shafts to draw it away. Just then 78 came thundering over the trestle spouting smoke, and suddenly began blowing for Maitland. Old Man Anderson became so frightened he ran away with the wagon through the woods and tore it up worse than the horse ever could have done. He doesn't know yet what a train looks like, and says he doesn't care.

VOCABULARY

patronage—being mean; talking down to someone.
ridicule—teasing.
grove—group of trees with open ground between them.
belched—gushed forth.
spouting—shooting out.

stop+think

What is unusual about the man in "The Way of a Man with a Train"?

....

....

....

....

GATHER YOUR THOUGHTS

A. COMPARE AND CONTRAST In what ways are the characters from "The Eatonville Anthology" similar? In what ways are they different?

1. Use the diagram below to help you compare and contrast the characters.

2. Use the center part to list the things that all 3 characters have in common.

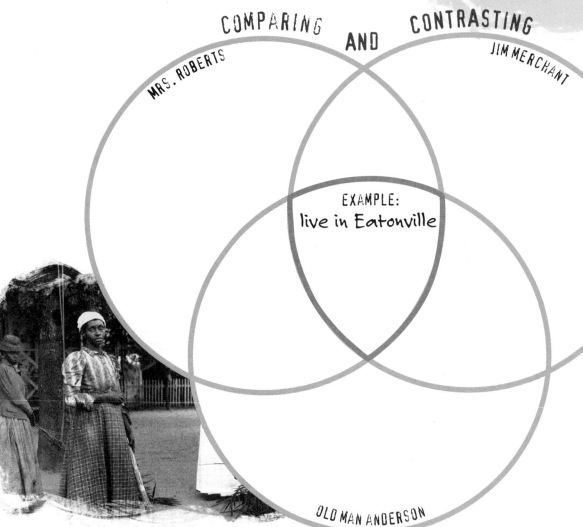

COMPARING AND CONTRASTING

MRS. ROBERTS

JIM MERCHANT

EXAMPLE:
live in Eatonville

OLD MAN ANDERSON

B. CHOOSE A SUBJECT Prepare to write a dialogue. Think about which of the 3 characters above you liked the most. Write the name of the character and 3 questions you would like to ask him or her.

CHARACTER

#1

#2

#3

IV. WRITE

Pretend you meet one of Hurston's characters. Imagine a conversation and write a brief **dialogue**.

1. Model your writing style on Hurston's style.
2. Remember to ask the character at least 1 of the questions you wrote on the previous page. Make the conversation sound like real people talking.
3. Use the Writers' Checklist to help you revise.

A Conversation Between

and

_____

_____

_____

_____

_____

_____

_____

_____

V. WRAP-UP

What do you think of the writing style of "The Eatonville Anthology"?

_____

_____

_____

_____

_____

_____

_____

_____

_____

_____

Playfulness

Support

Family Ties

Families are bound together by more than just blood. It is the multiple threads of love and loyalty that really create the family.

Love

Loyalty

When you were a young child, you probably enjoyed listening to stories read aloud. But reading aloud is helpful even for experienced readers. When you read aloud or listen to a story, you can get a better idea of the writer's style.

I. BEFORE YOU READ

Work with a partner.

1. One person should read aloud the first 2 paragraphs of the selection as the other listens. Then switch. Listen carefully to the kinds of words and images the writer uses.

"Visit to Africa" from *All God's Children Need Traveling Shoes* by Maya Angelou

The breezes of the West African night were intimate and shy, licking the hair, sweeping through cotton dresses with unseemly intimacy, then disappearing into the utter blackness. Daylight was equally insistent, but much more bold and thoughtless. It dazzled, muddling the sight. It forced through my closed eyelids, bringing me up and out of a borrowed bed and into brand new streets.

After living nearly two years in Cairo, I had brought my son Guy to enter the University of Ghana in Accra. I planned staying for two weeks with a friend of a colleague, settling Guy into his dormitory, then continuing to Liberia to a job with the Department of Information.

VOCABULARY
intimacy—familiarity; closeness.
Cairo—capital of Egypt.
Accra—seaport city of Ghana, in western Africa.
Liberia—country in western Africa.

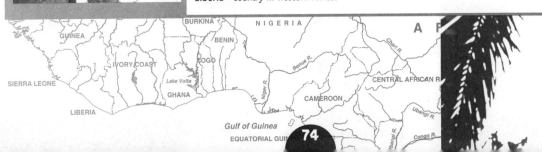

2. What did you notice about the selection? Complete the sentence and then share your thoughts with a partner.

The author's writing style is . . .

READ

Read the rest of the selection at your own pace.
1. As you read, stop to **predict** what will happen next.
2. Use the Response Notes to jot down anything that confuses or surprises you.

"Visit to Africa" continued

Guy was seventeen and quick. I was thirty-three and determined. We were Black Americans in West Africa, where for the first time in our lives the color of our skin was accepted as correct and normal.

Guy had finished high school in Egypt, his Arabic was good and his health excellent. He assured me that he would quickly learn a Ghanaian language, and he certainly could look after himself. I had worked successfully as a journalist in Cairo, and failed sadly at a marriage which I ended with false public dignity and copious secret tears. But with all crying in the past, I was on my way to another adventure. The future was plump with promise.

For two days Guy and I laughed. We looked at the Ghanaian streets and laughed. We listened to the melodious languages and laughed. We looked at each other and laughed out loud.

RESPONSE NOTES

EXAMPLE:
Interesting! Bet something bad will happen.

VOCABULARY
journalist—person whose job is gathering, writing, and presenting the news.
copious—more than enough; abundant.
plump—pleasantly round and full.
melodious—sweet-sounding; pleasing to the ear.

RESPONSE NOTES

On the third day, Guy, on a pleasure outing, was injured in an automobile accident. One arm and one leg were fractured and his neck was broken.

STOP AND PREDICT

What do you think will happen next?

STOP AND PREDICT

STOP AND PREDICT

July and August of 1962 stretched out like fat men yawning after a <u>sumptuous</u> dinner. They had every right to gloat, for they had eaten me up. <u>Gobbled</u> me down. <u>Consumed</u> my spirit, not in a wild rush, but slowly, with the <u>obscene</u> patience of certain victors. I became a shadow walking in the white hot streets, and a dark specter in the hospital.

There was no solace in knowing that the doctors and nurses hovering around Guy were African, nor in the company of the Black American <u>expatriates</u> who, hearing of our misfortune, came to share some of the slow hours. Racial loyalties and cultural attachments had become meaningless.

Trying utterly, I could not match Guy's stoicism. He lay calm, week after week, in a prison of plaster from which only his face and one leg and arm were visible.

VOCABULARY
sumptuous—costly; magnificent.
Gobbled—ate fast and greedily.
Consumed—used up; spent.
obscene—impure; indecent.
expatriates—people living outside their own country.

"Visit to Africa" continued

His assurances that he would heal and be better than new drove me into a faithless silence. Had I been less timid, I would have cursed God. Had I come from a different background, I would have gone further and denied His very existence. Having neither the courage nor the historical precedent, I raged inside myself like a blinded bull in a metal stall.

STOP AND PREDICT STOP AND PREDICT

What do you think will happen to Guy?

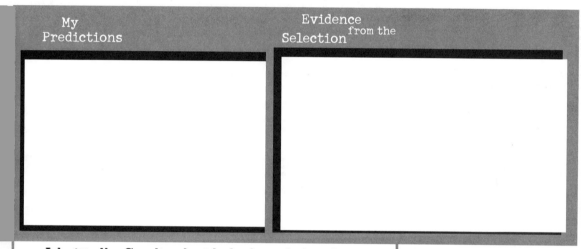

My Predictions	Evidence from the Selection

Admittedly, Guy lived with the knowledge that an unexpected and very hard sneeze could force the fractured <u>vertebrae</u> against his <u>spinal cord</u>, and he would be paralyzed or die immediately, but he had only an <u>infatuation</u> with life. He hadn't lived long enough to fall in love with this brutally delicious experience. He could lightly waft away to another place, if there really was another place, where his youthful innocence would assure him a crown, wings, a harp, <u>ambrosia</u>, free milk and an absence of <u>nostalgic</u> yearning. (I was raised on

VOCABULARY
vertebrae—bones that form the backbone.
spinal cord—thick nerve tissue that goes from the brain down through the backbone.
infatuation—exaggerated fondness or passion; foolish love.
ambrosia—food of the gods.
nostalgic—affectionate longing for one's home, country, or things from long ago.

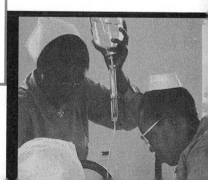

RESPONSE NOTES

the spirituals which ached to "See my old mother in glory" or "Meet with my dear children in heaven," but even the most fanciful lyricists never dared to suggest that those cavorting souls gave one thought to those of us left to moil in the world.) My wretchedness reminded me that, on the other hand, I would be rudderless.

I had lived with family until my son was born in my sixteenth year. When he was two months old and perched on my left hip, we left my mother's house and together, save for one year when I was touring, we had been each other's home and center for seventeen years. He could die if he wanted to and go off to wherever dead folks go, but I, I would be left without a home.

VOCABULARY
lyricists—people who write the words for a song.
cavorting—prancing or jumping about.
moil—work hard.

STOP AND REFLECT STOP AND REFLECT

Which of your predictions were "true"?

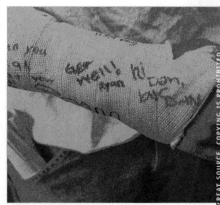

GATHER YOUR THOUGHTS

SUMMARIZE "What is this selection all about?" Your answer to that question could be a paragraph or two of summary.

1. Start with a sentence that tells the main idea, the point the writer is trying to make. Ask yourself what Maya Angelou wants readers to remember. Write the main idea in the top space.

2. In the boxes under the main idea, list details from the text that support the main idea.

MAIN IDEA

SUPPORTING DETAIL

SUPPORTING DETAIL

SUPPORTING DETAIL

SUPPORTING DETAIL

IV. WRITE

Write a **summary** of the selection. Imagine that your summary is appearing on a new book jacket for Angelou's writing.

1. Start with the main idea sentence you wrote.

2. Use the Writers' Checklist to help you revise.

V. WRAP-UP

What did you learn from reading "Visit to Africa"?

Before you read something new, skim the title and selection. Ask yourself, "What is this about? What do I already know about this? What experiences have I had related to it?" That way you will be prepared for what you are reading.

BEFORE YOU READ

Look at the titles and briefly skim through the poems.

1. Think about what these poems are about. (*Tía* is the Spanish word for "aunt.")

2. Explore your own ideas about family ties. On the arms of the Word Web, write words and phrases that reveal your own ideas about family ties.

WORD WEB

FAMILY TIES

READ

Read both poems at your own pace.

1. Write any **reactions** or comments you have in the Response Notes.

2. As you read, use a double-entry journal to list and write about lines and phrases from the poems that you find interesting.

"Dear Tía" and "Papa" by Carolina Hospital

DEAR TÍA

I do not write.
The years have frightened me away.
My life in a land so familiarly <u>foreign</u>,
a <u>denial</u> of your <u>presence</u>.
Your name is mine.
One black and white photograph of your youth,
all I hold on to.
One story of your past.
The pain comes not from <u>nostalgia.</u>
I do not miss your voice urging me in play,
your smiles,
or your pride when others called you my mother.
I cannot close my eyes and feel your soft skin;
listen to you laughter;
smell the sweetness of your bath.
I write because I cannot remember at all.

VOCABULARY
foreign—of or from another country.
denial—refusal to accept or believe something.
presence—immediate nearness.
nostalgia—bittersweet longing for things, persons, or situations of the past.

DOUBLE-ENTRY JOURNAL

QUOTE	MY THOUGHTS
"One black and white photograph of your youth, all I hold on to."	

RESPONSE NOTES

Papa

The two sat on the shoreline
under a piercing sun
ignoring the calls of their children
begging them to join them in play.
Both shared moments never lived
as wrinkled bodies crossed them
offering advice.
Without a glance they continued
almost whispering about a sacred man,
an outcast of their past,
an omen in their future.

VOCABULARY
piercing—penetrating; in this case, hot.
sacred—godly; holy.

DOUBLE-ENTRY JOURNAL

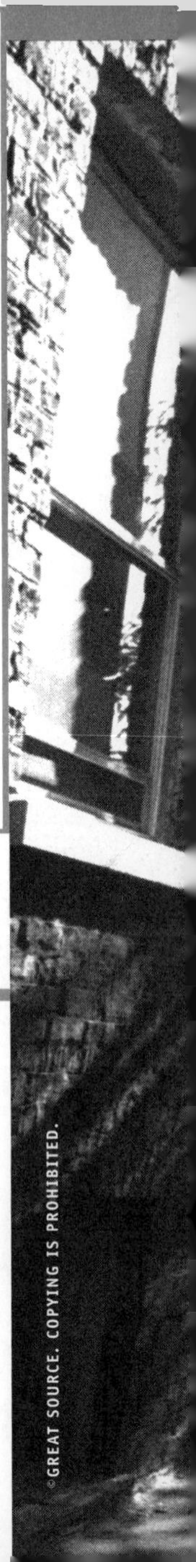

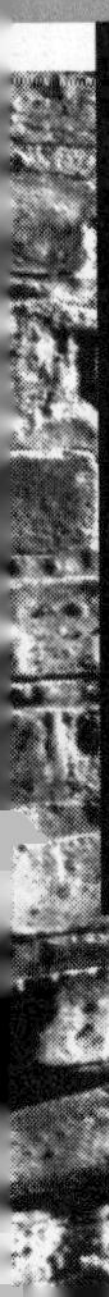

QUOTE	MY THOUGHTS
"Both shared moments never lived"	

GATHER YOUR THOUGHTS

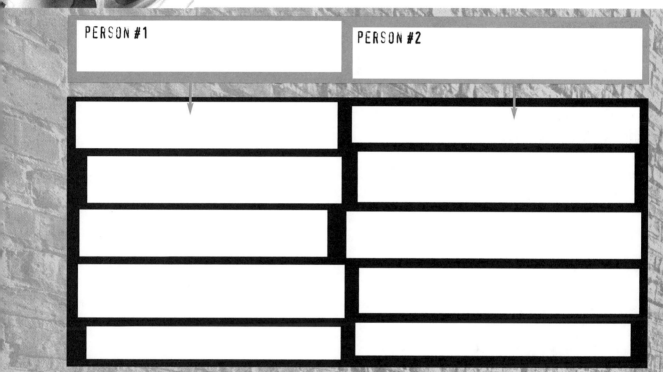

A. BRAINSTORM IDEAS Use the poem "Papa" as a model for a poem of your own about 2 members of your family.

1. Select the 2 people you want to write about (such as you and your mother, your aunt and your grandfather, two cousins). Write the 2 people's names in the top boxes below.

2. Brainstorm words that you associate with these two people— their characteristics, appearances, hobbies, favorite things, and so on. List the words in the bottom boxes.

PERSON #1

PERSON #2

B. USE A MODEL Like the poem "Papa," your poem will be 3 sentences.

1. The first sentence should begin just as "Papa" does with the words "The two sat."

2. Complete that sentence in 3 different ways. Use your brainstorming ideas above to help you set the scene of where the two people are and what they're doing.

#1 The two sat

#2 The two sat

#3 The two sat

IV. WRITE

Write your own **poem** to show your feelings and ideas about 2 members of your family.

1. The poem should begin with the words "The two sat" and be 3 sentences in length.

2. Remember to title your poem.

3. Use the Writers' Checklist to help you revise.

V. WRAP-UP

What does Carolina Hospital say about family ties in her poems?

Stories of the Arab World

More than 200 million Arabs live in the Arab World, which
spreads across the Middle East, southwest Asia, and northern
Africa. Despite this vast extent of land, Arabs are united by
a shared history, culture, and literature.

9: The Guest Who Ran Away

What does it mean to "read between the lines"? Sometimes the author will tell everything you need to know about a character. Other times you will need to read between the lines and make inferences (reasonable guesses).

BEFORE YOU READ

Look at the title and author's name and read the first paragraph.
1. Begin thinking about the characters and what they are like.
2. Answer the 4 questions below about the story.

"The Guest Who Ran Away"

A TUNISIAN FOLK TALE RETOLD BY INEA BUSHNAQ

A weary traveler stopped at a <u>Bedouin's</u> tent and asked for shelter for the night. Without delay the man killed a couple of chickens and handed them to his wife to <u>stew</u> for their guest's supper.

▼ VOCABULARY
Bedouin's—belonging to an Arab who wanders in the desert.
stew—cook by boiling slowly.

Preview

1. **What did you find out from reading the title and author's name?**

....

2. **What did you learn by reading the first paragraph?**

....

3. **What characters are involved?**

....

4. **What do you think this story will be about?**

....

....

READ

Read the rest of "The Guest Who Ran Away."

1. Circle actions or words that seem important to understanding the characters.

2. Clarify what's happening by numbering key events in the Response Notes.

"The Guest Who Ran Away" continued

As the woman stirred the meat in her copper cooking pot, she smelled the rich steam and (could not resist tasting a piece) to see if it was soft. But mouthful followed mouthful, and soon nothing was left of the two birds but one neck. This she gave to her little son to nibble. The boy found it so savory that he whined, "Give me some, Mother, give me some!" The woman slapped the little boy and scolded him: "It's a shameful habit your father taught you; enough of it, I tell you!"

Response Notes

EXAMPLE:

1. Wife eats what she's cooking.

clarify + predict

Why does the woman eat all the chicken? What does this tell you about her?

....

....

What do you predict the woman will do now that she has no dinner for the guest?

....

....

clarify + predict

On the other side of the woven hanging which screened the women's part of the tent from the rest, the traveler overheard this exchange. "What habit has his father taught your child?" he asked curiously. "Oh,"

VOCABULARY
nibble—eat with small, quick bites.
savory—tasty; pleasing.
woven—made by passing threads over and under one another to make a fabric.
exchange—trade in goods or information.

said the woman, "whenever a guest arrives at our tent, he cuts off his ears and roasts them over the fire for my son to eat." Making not a sound, the traveler picked up his shoes and fled.

Why does the woman lie to the guest?

_____

_____

_____

"What ails our guest? Why has he left in such a hurry?" asked the Bedouin, entering the tent soon after. "A fine guest indeed!" exclaimed his wife. "He <u>snatched</u> the chickens out of my pot and ran away!" <u>Hitching</u> up his robes, the Bedouin gave chase, shouting, "Let me have one, at least; you may keep the other!" But his guest only ran faster.

VOCABULARY
snatched—grabbed quickly.
Hitching—raising or pulling up.

Summarize

Which of your predictions turned out to be right? Which were way off? Explain here.

_____

_____

_____

_____

_____

GATHER YOUR THOUGHTS

A. USE GRAPHIC ORGANIZERS Think carefully about the woman in "The Guest Who Ran Away." The author tells you little about her. It's your job to make inferences about her character. Use the Character Attribute Map below to "read between the lines."

Character Attribute Map

DIRECTIONS: Identify 4 qualities of the woman. Put a different quality in each box. Then find examples from the story that support your description.

#1_____
EXAMPLES:

#2_____
EXAMPLES:

The Woman

#3_____
EXAMPLES:

#4_____
EXAMPLES:

B. PLAN Now plan a short folk tale of your own. You can use Bushnaq's characters or invent some yourself. Begin by making some notes here.

Who are the characters?

Where does the story take place?

When does the story take place?

What happens in the story?

Why does it happen?

WRITE

Think of how your folk tale will start. Write the **story beginning**.

1. Try to establish the who, what, where, when, and why of your story.

2. Use the Writers' Checklist to help you revise.

Title: _____

_____

_____

_____

_____

_____

_____

_____

_____

_____

_____

_____

_____

_____

_____

_____

**WRITERS'
CHECKLIST**

COMMA SPLICES

☐ Did you avoid comma splices?
A comma splice occurs when two simple sentences are joined with just a comma.

EXAMPLE: *The man was tricky, he lied a lot.*
To correct a comma splice, insert a comma plus a joining word (*and, or, but, so*) or a semicolon (;). Another option is to make two sentences.

EXAMPLES: *The man was tricky,* **and** *he lied a lot.* *The man was tricky; he lied a lot. The man was tricky. He lied a lot.*

_____

_____

_____

_____

_____

_____

_____

_____

_____

_____

_____

_____

_____

_____

_____

V. WRAP-UP

What part of "The Guest Who Ran Away" did you like most? Why?

_____

_____

_____

_____

_____

_____

_____

_____

READERS' CHECKLIST

ENJOYMENT
- ❏ Did you like the reading?
- ❏ Was the reading experience pleasurable?
- ❏ Would you want to reread the piece or recommend it to someone?

10

The Price of Pride and How Si' Djeha Staved Off Hunger

When you ask what a story is about, you're asking about plot. Plot is the action of a story. It is the sequence of events that moves the story from start to finish. Every plot has a conflict. The conflict is the major problem or concern in the story.

I. BEFORE YOU READ

Think about the titles of the 2 stories below.

1. Make predictions about what you think the conflict or problem will be in both stories.
2. Record your predictions in the middle column of the chart.
3. Fill in the column on the right after you've finished reading the stories.

Predict

STORY	WHAT I THINK THE CONFLICT WILL BE	WHAT THE CONFLICT ACTUALLY IS
"THE PRICE OF PRIDE"		
"HOW SI' DJEHA STAVED OFF HUNGER"		

READ

With a partner, take turns reading these 2 stories aloud to each other.

1. Make notes in the margin whenever something new happens in the plot.

2. Use the Response Notes to **predict** what will happen next.

"The Price of Pride"

A SAUDI ARABIAN FOLK TALE RETOLD BY INEA BUSHNAQ

A <u>Bedouin</u> once had business in the cattle market of a town. He took his young son with him, but in the confusion of the place he lost track of his boy and the child was stolen.

The father hired a <u>crier</u> to shout through the streets that a reward of one thousand <u>piasters</u> was offered for the return of the child. Although the man who held the boy heard the crier, greed had opened his belly and he hoped to earn an even larger sum. So he waited and said nothing.

On the following day the crier was sent through the streets again. But this time the sum he offered was five hundred piasters, not a thousand. The <u>kidnapper</u> still held out. To his surprise, on the third day the crier offered a mere one hundred piasters. He hurried to return the boy and collect his reward. Curious, he asked the father why the sum of money had <u>dwindled</u> from day to day.

> EXAMPLE:
> boy is stolen—maybe man won't get money

VOCABULARY

Bedouin—Arab who wanders in the desert.
crier—official who announces the orders of a court of law.
piasters—money used in Egypt, Lebanon, Libya, Sudan, Syria, and Turkey.
kidnapper—someone who takes or holds another by force.
dwindled—lessened; gone down.

"The Price of Pride" continued

The father said, "On the first day my son was angry and refused to eat your food; is that not so?" "Yes," agreed the kidnapper. "On the second day he took a little, and on the last he asked for bread of his own accord," said the father. It had been so, the kidnapper agreed. "Well," said the father, "As I judge it, that first day my son was as <u>unblemished</u> as refined gold. Like a man of honor, he refused to break bread with his <u>captor</u>. To bring him back with his pride <u>untarnished</u>, I was ready to pay one thousand piasters. On the second day, when hunger made him forget the conduct of a nobleman, he accepted food at your table, and I offered five hundred piasters for him. But when he had been reduced to begging humbly for food, his return was worth but one hundred piasters to me."

Storyboard

Retell in your own words the plot of this story.

1.

2.

3.

VOCABULARY
unblemished—lacking in guilt, without fault.
captor—person who holds someone prisoner.
untarnished—not damaged.

"How Si' Djeha Staved Off Hunger"

AN ALGERIAN FOLK TALE RETOLD BY INEA BUSHNAQ

Once Si' Djeha was traveling across a stretch of desert. His throat was <u>parched</u> and his belt was slipping way below his hips, for it had been many hours since he had eaten. At last, in the distance, resting in the slim shadow of a rock, he saw another traveler eating his midday meal. Si' Djeha's spirits rose, and in no time he was <u>squatting</u> in the shade beside the traveler.

"Where do you come from?" asked the man.

"From your very own village," said Si' Djeha accommodatingly.

"May your news be good news, brother," said the man.

"As good as you could wish for," Si' Djeha assured him.

VOCABULARY
parched—dry.
squatting—sitting on one's heels.

"Tell me about my wife Umm Othman."

"Plump and healthy as a duck."

"And Othman, my son?"

"In the coffeehouse beating his friends at backgammon."

"And the camel?"

"So fat it will surely burst."

"How about my dog?"

"Watchful as ever."

"And the house?"

"Like a fortress."

Storyboard

Retell what has happened so far in the plot of this story.

1.

2.

3.

VOCABULARY
backgammon—board game for two people.

"How Si' Djeha Staved Off Hunger" continued

Satisfied, the man fell silent and returned to his meal. Si' Djeha waited hopefully, but the man did not invite him to share the food. Then suddenly Si' Djeha jumped up.

"Where are you off to in such a hurry?" asked the man.

"I must return to the village. Since your dog died, the robbers have become quite a <u>plague</u>."

"My dog dead?"

"Yes."

"How did he die?"

"He must have eaten too much of the flesh of your camel."

"My camel dead?"

"Yes."

"How did it die?"

"It tripped over Umm Othman's tomb."

"My wife dead?"

"Yes.

"How did she die?"

"Of a broken heart over Othman's death."

"My son dead?"

"Yes."

"How did he die?"

"He was buried in the <u>rubble</u> when the house collapsed."

VOCABULARY

plague—problem that occurs time and time again; persistent annoyance.
rubble—broken or crumbled material.

"How Si' Djeha Staved Off Hunger" continued

At that the man began to tear his hair and roar as if he were mad and ran off to the village as fast as he could.

Meanwhile Si' Djeha drew back his right sleeve, invoked the name of Allah the Merciful and the Compassionate, and reached for his dinner.

Reflect

What, in your own words, was "How Si' Djeha Staved Off Hunger" about?

....

....

....

....

Were you surprised by how this story ended? Explain.

....

....

....

....

....

Go back to page 94 and complete the right-hand column about the conflict in each story.

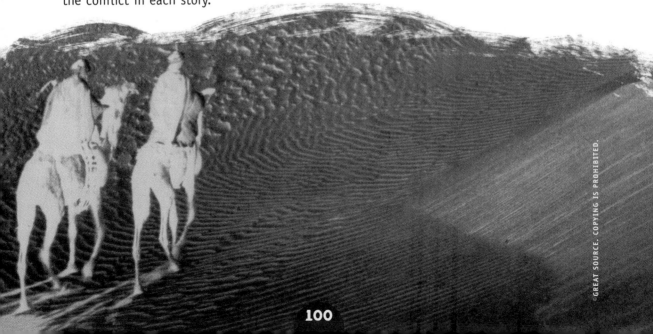

GATHER YOUR THOUGHTS

A. DISCUSS AND REFLECT Take time to think about and discuss with a partner the folk tales you just read. Then answer these questions.

1. What is the conflict in the plot of "The Price of Pride"?

2. What is the conflict in the plot of "How Si' Djeha Staved Off Hunger"?

B. END A STORY Along with creating a conflict, writers usually solve it. In "The Guest Who Ran Away," the conflict occurs when the woman eats the guest's supper. The conflict is resolved when she makes up a story to hide her greed, and the guest runs away.

1. How is the conflict or problem solved in "The Price of Pride"?

2. How is the conflict or problem solved in "How Si' Djeha Staved Off Hunger"?

C. ORGANIZE THE STORY Use the boxes below to show the sequence of events in 1 of the folk tales you just read.

1. Use the first box to tell what happens first. Use the second box to tell what happens next, and so on.

2. Put a star by the box where the conflict is solved.

1.

2.

3.

4.

5.

WRITE

Now return to the folk tale you began in the last lesson. How will it end? Write the **story ending**.

1. Be sure you provide a solution to the main conflict.

2. Use the Writers' Checklist to help you revise.

Continue your writing on the next page.

WRITERS' CHECKLIST

RUN-ONS

❑ Did you avoid writing run-on sentences? The two parts of a compound sentence must be joined by a comma and a conjunction such as *and* or *but*. A compound sentence that is missing the joining word and the comma is called a run-on sentence.

EXAMPLE: *He read the story it was great.*

You can fix a run-on by breaking it apart into two sentences or by inserting a comma and a joining word in the correct spot.

EXAMPLE: *He read the story, and it was great.*

Continue your writing from the previous page.

_____

_____

_____

_____

_____

_____

_____

V. WRAP-UP

What made "The Price of Pride" and "How Si' Djeha Staved Off Hunger" easy or difficult to read?

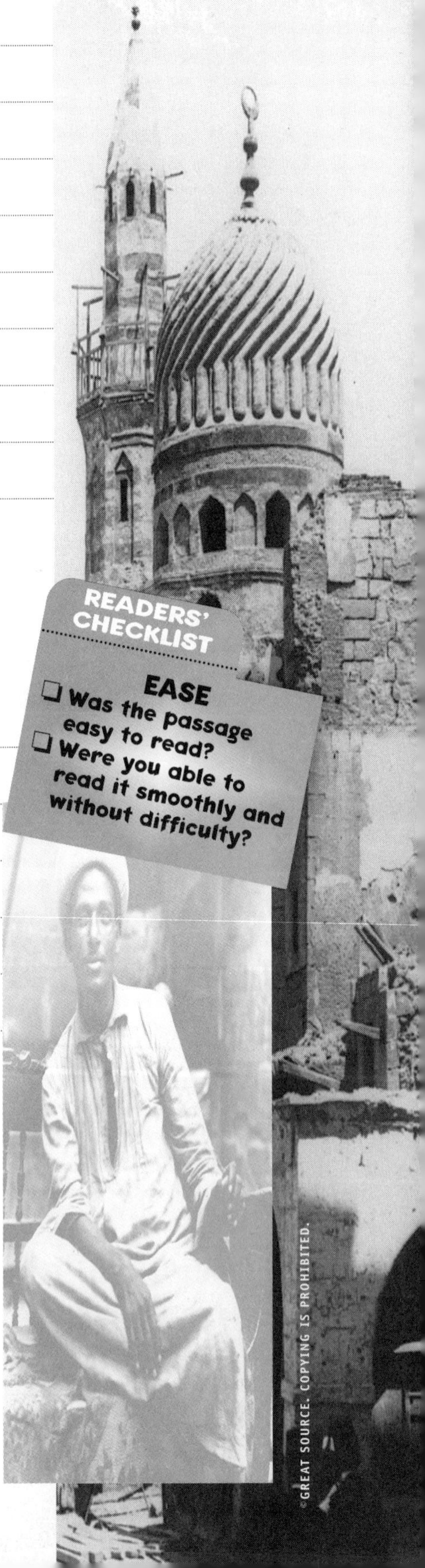

_____

_____

_____

_____

_____

Piri Thomas

Piri Thomas (1928–) was born to Puerto Rican and Cuban parents. He grew up poor in New York City but overcame a troubled childhood. As a poet, writer, and storyteller, Thomas focuses on people's struggles for survival and recognition and the damaging effects of racism.

Piri Thomas

PIRI THOMAS
DOWN THESE MEAN STREETS
A stunning autobiography of corruption and innocence

11: Puerto Rican Paradise

Seeing is believing. When you see illustrations or photographs, look them over before you read. Think to yourself, "What is this about? What do these illustrations tell me?"

I. BEFORE YOU READ

"Walk through" the pictures in the selection.
1. Think about how these images make you feel and what they make you think about.
2. Complete the sentences and record your thoughts and questions below.

PICTURE WALK

The illustrations make me feel . . .

They make me think about . . .

What do you think "Puerto Rican Paradise" is about? What questions do you have about it?

Read this part of Piri Thomas's memoir at your own pace.
1. As you read, **mark** or **highlight** the major events of the story.
2. Number and summarize them in the Response Notes.

"Puerto Rican Paradise" from *Down These Mean Streets*
by Piri Thomas

RESPONSE NOTES

Poppa didn't talk to me the next day. Soon he didn't talk much to anyone. He lost his night job—I forget why, and probably it was worth forgetting—and went back on home relief. It was 1941, and the Great Hunger called <u>Depression</u> was still down on Harlem.

But there was still the good old <u>WPA</u>. If a man was poor enough, he could dig a ditch for the government. Now Poppa was poor enough again.

The weather turned cold one more time, and so did our apartment. In the summer the cooped-up apartments in Harlem seem to catch all the heat and improve on it. It's the same in the winter. The cold, plastered walls embrace that cold from outside and make it a part of the apartment, till you don't know whether it's better to freeze out in the snow or by the stove, where four jets, wide open, <u>spout</u> <u>futile</u>, blue-yellow flames. It's hard on the rats, too.

Snow was falling. "My *Cristo*," Momma said, "<u>qué frío</u>. Doesn't that landlord have any <u>corazón</u>? Why don't he give more heat?" I wondered how Pops was making out working a pick and shovel in that falling snow.

EXAMPLE:
1. Poppa losing job means less money.

VOCABULARY
Depression—period of economic hard times during the 1930s.
WPA—Works Projects Administration, a government-sponsored job program.
spout—gush forth.
futile—useless.
qué frío—Spanish for "it's cold."
corazón—Spanish for "heart."

Momma picked up a hammer and began to beat the beat-up radiator that's copped a plea from so many beatings. Poor steam radiator, how could it give out heat when it was freezing itself? The hollow sounds Momma beat out of it brought echoes from other freezing people in the building. Everybody picked up the beat and it seemed a crazy, good idea. If everybody took turns beating on the radiators, everybody could keep warm from the exercise.

We drank hot cocoa and talked about summertime. Momma talked about Puerto Rico and how great it was, and how she'd like to go back one day, and how it was warm all the time there and no matter how poor you were over there, you could always live on green bananas, bacalao, and rice and beans. "Díos mío," she said, "I don't think I'll ever see my island again."

Look at the events you marked or highlighted. Write the 3 most important events.

TAKE NOTES

1.

2.

3.

"Sure you will, Mommie," said Miriam, my kid sister. She was eleven. "Tell us, tell us all about Porto Rico."

"It's not Porto Rico, it's Puerto Rico," said Momma.

"Tell us, Moms," said nine-year-old James, "about Puerto Rico."

VOCABULARY
radiator—heating device, often a metal piece next to a wall or window.
Puerto Rico—island in the Caribbean Sea, once owned by the Spanish, and later given to the U.S in 1898.
bacalao—type of fish.
Díos Mío—Spanish for "Oh, my God."

RESPONSE NOTES

"Yeah, Mommie," said six-year-old José.

Even the baby, Paulie, smiled.

Moms copped that wet-eyed look and began to dream-talk about her *isla verde*, Moses' land of milk and honey.

"When I was a little girl," she said, "I remember the getting up in the morning and getting the water from the river and getting the wood for the fire and the quiet of the greenlands and the golden color of the morning sky, the grass wet from the *lluvia* . . . *Ai, Díos*, the *coquís and the pajaritos making all the música* . . ."

"Mommie, were you poor?" asked Miriam.

"*Sí, muy pobre*, but very happy. I remember the hard work and the very little bit we had, but it was a good little bit. It counted very much. Sometimes when you have too much, the good gets lost within and you have to look very hard. But when you have a little, then the good does not have to be looked for so hard."

"Moms," I asked, "did everybody love each other—I mean, like if everybody was worth something, not like if some weren't important because they were poor—you know what I mean?"

"*Bueno hijo*, you have people everywhere who, because they have more, don't remember those who have very little. But in Puerto Rico those around you share *la pobreza* with you and they love you, because only poor people can understand poor people. I like *los Estados Unidos*, but it's sometimes a cold place to live— not because of the winter and the landlord not giving heat but because of the snow in the hearts of the people."

"Moms, didn't our people have any money or land?" I leaned forward, hoping to hear that my ancestors were noble princes born in Spain.

VOCABULARY

isla verde—Spanish for "green island," referring to Puerto Rico.
lluvia—Spanish for "rain."
coquís and the *pajaritos* making all the *música*—tiny frogs common to Puerto Rico. They, along with the small birds of the island, make much music.
Bueno hijo—Spanish for "Well, son."
la pobreza—Spanish for "poverty."
los Estados Unidos—Spanish for the "United States."

"Your grandmother and grandfather had a lot of land, but they lost that."

"How come, Moms?"

"Well, in those days there was nothing of what you call <u>contratos</u>, and when you bought or sold something, it was on your word and a handshake, and that's the way your <u>abuelos</u> bought their land and then lost it."

"Is that why we ain't got nuttin' now?" James asked pointedly.

"Oh, it—"

Write 3 things Momma remembers from her life in Puerto Rico.

TAKE NOTES

1.

2.

3.

The door opened and put an end to the kitchen <u>yak</u>. It was Poppa coming home from work. He came into the kitchen and brought all the cold with him. Poor Poppa, he looked so lost in the clothes he had on. A jacket and coat, sweaters on top of sweaters, two pairs of long johns, two pairs of pants, two pairs of socks, and a woolen cap. And under all that he was cold. His eyes were cold; his ears were red with pain. He took off his gloves and his fingers were stiff with cold.

"<u>¿Cómo está</u>?" said Momma. "I will make you coffee."

Poppa said nothing. His eyes were running hot frozen tears. He worked his fingers and rubbed his ears, and

VOCABULARY
contratos—Spanish for "contracts" or "written agreements."
abuelos—Spanish for "grandparents."
yak—slang for "talk."
¿Cómo está?—Spanish for "How are you?"

"Puerto Rican Paradise" CONTINUED

the pain made him make faces. "Get me some snow, Piri," he said finally.

I ran to the window, opened it, and scraped all the snow on the sill into one big snowball and brought it to him. We all watched in frozen wonder as Poppa took that snow and rubbed it on his ears and hands.

"Gee, Pops, don't it hurt?" I asked.

"Sí, but it's good for it. It hurts a little first, but it's good for the frozen parts."

I wondered why.

"How was it today?" Momma asked.

"Cold . . . ice cold."

Gee, I thought, *I'm sorry for you, Pops. You gotta suffer like this.*

"It was not always like this," my father said to the cold walls. "It's all the fault of the . . . depression."

Now place the most important story events on the timeline.

REMEMBER: The events on a timeline are in chronological, or time, order. Put the event that happened first on the far left (#1), and the event that happened last on the far right (#6).

TIMELINE

1.

3.

5.

2.

4.

6.

GATHER YOUR THOUGHTS

A. NARROW THE TOPIC Imagine that a friend asks you, "What is the story 'Puerto Rican Paradise' about?"

Now narrow a topic to write an autobiographical paragraph. Start with a broad topic and fine tune it.

A family

The answer "a family" is broad. It covers many more stories than this one.

My family

Family who moves to the U.S.

That still is not narrow enough.

Puerto Rican family in the U.S. during the Depression and the lessons learned about hard work

Now the topic has been narrowed.

B. DEVELOP THE TOPIC Next develop your narrowed topic. Tell the details that bring your topic to life. Put the events in order.

1.

2.

3.

4.

IV. WRITE

Develop your notes into an **autobiographical paragraph**.

1. Start with a topic sentence that grabs the readers attention.

2. Use transition words to help ideas flow smoothly (later, then, although, for instance).

3. Use the Writers' Checklist to help you revise.

WRITERS' CHECKLIST

CAPITALIZATION

❑ **Did you capitalize titles? Capitalize titles used before a name and titles used to directly address someone.**
EXAMPLES: *President Lincoln, Dr. Jacqueline Schaefer, First Sargent Joseph Pawlisz, Yes, Mother*

❑ **Did you capitalize the names of specific places? Capitalize the names of continents, countries, states, cities, and counties. Capitalize the names of specific regions, bodies of water, topographical features (e.g., mountain ranges), and streets.**
EXAMPLES: *South America, Puerto Rico, Colorado, Kane County, Pacific Ocean, Rocky Mountains, Rush Street, Mississippi River*

V. WRAP-UP

What did you think about the author's writing style in "Puerto Rican Paradise"?

READERS' CHECKLIST

STYLE

- ❑ **Did you find the passage well written?**
- ❑ **Are the sentences well constructed and the words well chosen?**
- ❑ **Does the style show you how to be a better writer?**

12: **If You Ain't Got Heart, You Ain't Got Nada**

Do you have "conversations" with writers and their works? Doing so helps you become more involved in what you are reading. Writing out your thoughts helps you explore your ideas as you read.

BEFORE YOU READ

Read the title and first few paragraphs of the selection.
1. As you read, circle any words or phrases that stand out for you. What do you want to ask or say to Piri Thomas?
2. Then complete the quickwrite on the next page.

"If You Ain't Got Heart, You Ain't Got Nada"
from *Down These Mean Streets* by Piri Thomas

We were moving—our new pad was back in <u>Spanish Harlem</u>—to 104th Street between Lex and Park Avenue.

Moving into a new block is a big jump for a Harlem kid. You're torn up from your hard-won turf and brought into an "I don't know you" block where every kid is some kind of enemy. Even when the block belongs to your own people, you are still an outsider who has to prove himself a down stud with heart.

As the moving van rolled to a stop in front of our new building, number 109, we were all standing there, waiting for it—Momma, Poppa, Sis, Paulie, James, José, and myself. I made out like I didn't notice the cats looking us over, especially me—I was gang age. I read their faces and found no trust, plenty of suspicion, and a glint of rising hate. I said to myself, *These cats don't*

VOCABULARY
Spanish Harlem—area in New York City where many Spanish-speaking people live.

mean nothin'. They're just nosy. But I remembered what had happened to me in my old block, and that it had ended with me in the hospital.

This was a tough-looking block. That was good, that was cool; but my old turf had been tough, too. *I'm tough,* a voice within said. *I hope I'm tough enough. I am tough enough. I've got* mucho corazón, *I'm king wherever I go. I'm a killer to my heart. I not only can live, I will live, no punk out, no die out, walk bad; be down, cool breeze, smooth.* My mind raced, and thoughts crashed against each other, trying to <u>reassemble</u> themselves into a pattern of rep. I turned slowly and with eyelids half-closed I looked at the rulers of this new world and with a cool shrug of my shoulders I followed the movers into the hallway of number 109 and dismissed the coming war from my mind.

VOCABULARY
reassemble—to come together again.

QUICKWRITE

NOW QUICKWRITE. WHAT DO YOU WANT TO ASK OR SAY TO THE AUTHOR? SHARE YOUR RESPONSE WITH A PARTNER.

READ

Read the rest of the story.
1. As you read, note the causes and effects.
2. Ask yourself, "What happened? Why did this happen?" Note your **reactions** to what happens in the Response Notes.

"If You Ain't Got Heart, You Ain't Got Nada" CONTINUED

The next morning I went to my new school, called Patrick Henry, and strange, mean eyes followed me.

"Say, pops," said a voice belonging to a guy I later came to know as Waneko, "where's your territory?"

In the same tone of voice Waneko had used, I answered, "I'm on it, dad, what's shaking?"

"Bad, huh?" He half-smiled.

"No—not all the way. Good when I'm cool breeze and bad when I'm down."

"What's your name, kid?"

"That depends. 'Piri' when I'm smooth and 'Johnny Gringo' when stomping time's around."

"What's your name now?" he pushed.

"You name me, man," I answered, playing my role like a champ.

He looked around, and with no kind of words, his boys cruised in. Guys I would come to know, to fight, to hate, to love, to take care of. Little Red, Waneko, Little Louie, Indio, Carlito, Alfredo, Crip, and plenty more. I stiffened and said to myself, *Stomping time, Piri boy, go with heart.*

I fingered the garbage-can handle in my pocket—my homemade brass <u>knuckles</u>. They were great for breaking down large odds into small, chopped-up ones.

Waneko, secure in his grandstand, said, "We'll name you later, <u>*panín*</u>."

I didn't answer. Scared, yeah, but wooden-faced to the end, I thought, <u>Chévere</u>, *panín*.

RESPONSE NOTES

EXAMPLE:
Must have been hard for Piri to calmly talk to him.

VOCABULARY
knuckles—joints that connect the fingers to the hand.
panín—Spanish term of affection, like "honey." Here it is used in a teasing way.
Chévere—Spanish for "cool."

STOP aND THiNK

Ask yourself, "What is happening in the story? Why is it happening?" Record 1 cause-and-effect relationship that you noticed.

CAUSE
WHY DID IT HAPPEN?
Waneko and his gang confront Piri.

- - →

EFFECT
WHAT HAPPENED?
Piri is afraid. He is prepared to fight.

CAUSE
WHY DID IT HAPPEN?

- - →

EFFECT
WHAT HAPPENED?

Now read the rest of the story.

RESPONSE NOTES

"If You Ain't Got Heart, You Ain't Got Nada" CONTINUED

It wasn't long in coming. Three days later, at about 6 p.m., Waneko and his boys were sitting around the <u>stoop</u> at number 115. 1 was cut off from my number 109. For an instant I thought, *Make a break for it down the basement steps and through the back yard—get away in one piece!* Then I thought, *Caramba! Live punk, dead hero. I'm no punk kid. I'm not copping any pleas.* I kept walking, hell's a-burning, hell's a-churning, rolling with cheer. *Walk on, baby man, roll on without fear. What's he going to call?*

"Whatta ya say, Mr. Johnny Gringo?" drawled Waneko.

Think, man, I told myself, *think your way out of a stomping. Make it good.* "I hear you 104th Street coolies are supposed to have heart," I said. "I don't know this for sure. You know there's a lot of streets where a whole 'click' is made out of punks who can't fight one guy unless they all jump him for the stomp." I hoped this

VOCABULARY
stoop—steps at the door of a house.

118

"If You Ain't Got Heart, You Ain't Got Nada" CONTINUED

would push Waneko into giving me a fair one. His
expression didn't change.

"Maybe we don't look at it that way."

Crazy, man. I cheer inwardly, the cabrón *is falling
into my setup. We'll see who gets messed up first, baby!*
"I wasn't talking to you," I said. "Where I come from, the
pres is president 'cause he got heart when it comes to
dealing."

Waneko was starting to look uneasy. He had bit on
my worm and felt like a sucker fish. His boys were now
light on me. They were no longer so much interested in
stomping me as in seeing the outcome between Waneko
and me. "Yeah," was his reply.

I smiled at him. "You trying to dig where I'm at and
now you got me interested in you. I'd like to see where
you're at."

Waneko hesitated a tiny little second before
replying.

"Yeah."

I knew I'd won. Sure, I'd have to fight; but one guy,
not ten or fifteen. If I lost I might still get stomped, and if
I won I might get stomped. I took care of this with my
next sentence. "I don't know you or your boys," I said,
"but they look cool to me. They don't feature as punks."

I had left him out purposely when I said "they." Now
his boys were in a separate class. I had cut him off. He
would have to fight me on his own, to prove his heart to
himself, to his boys, and most important, to his turf. He
got away from the stoop and asked, "Fair one, Gringo?"

"Uh-uh," I said, "roll all the way—anything goes." I
thought, *I've got to beat him bad and yet not bad enough
to take his prestige all away.* He had corazón. He came
on me. *Let him draw first blood,* I thought, *it's his block.*
Smish, my nose began to bleed. His boys cheered, his

VOCABULARY

expression—look on his face; way of showing thoughts or feelings.
cabrón—Spanish for "crazy goat."

heart cheered, his turf cheered. "Waste this chump," somebody shouted.

Okay, baby, now it's my turn. He swung. I grabbed innocently, and my forehead smashed into his nose. His eyes crossed. His fingernails went for my eye and landed in my mouth—crunch, I bit hard. I punched him in the mouth as he pulled away from me, and he slammed his foot into my chest.

We broke, my nose running red, my chest throbbing, his finger—well, that was his worry. I tied him up with body punching and slugging. We rolled onto the street. I wrestled for acceptance, he for rejection or, worse yet, acceptance on his terms. It was time to start peace talks. I smiled at him. "You got heart, baby," I said.

He answered with a punch to my head. I grunted and hit back, harder now. I had to back up my overtures of peace with strength. I bit him in the ribs, I rubbed my knuckles in his ear as we clinched. I tried again. "You deal good," I said.

"You too," he muttered, pressuring out. And just like that, the fight was over. No more words. We just separated, hands half up, half down. My heart pumped out, *You've established your rep. Move over, 104th Street. Lift your wings, I'm one of your baby chicks now.*

STOP AND THINK

Think to yourself, "What did Piri do? Why did he have to take these actions?" Describe 2 more cause-and-effect relationships.

CAUSE	EFFECT
WHY DID IT HAPPEN?	WHAT HAPPENED?

CAUSE	EFFECT
WHY DID IT HAPPEN?	WHAT HAPPENED?

GATHER YOUR THOUGHTS

A. DISCUSS Get together with others in a small group and review what people wrote in their Response Notes.
1. Compare your graphic organizers on causes and effects.
2. Answer these cause-and-effect questions.

Why does Piri have to prove himself?

Why do you think he fights in order to prove himself?

B. PLAN Now plan a narrative paragraph about a situation in which you had to prove something. Maybe, for instance, you had to prove to yourself that you could win a place on a team or that you weren't afraid of something.
1. Think about the experience.
2. Then write the causes and effects that were involved.

EXPERIENCE

CAUSES

1.

2.

3.

EFFECTS

1.

2.

3.

IV. WRITE

Write a **narrative paragraph** about an experience when you had to prove something to yourself.
1. Use a first-person point of view (*I* or *we*).
2. Use the Writers' Checklist to help you revise.

V. WRAP-UP

What did this story make you think about?

Dreams

Dreams give hope and provide a guiding light to our lives. People often dream the impossible—and sometimes achieve what seems impossible too.

Helen Keller

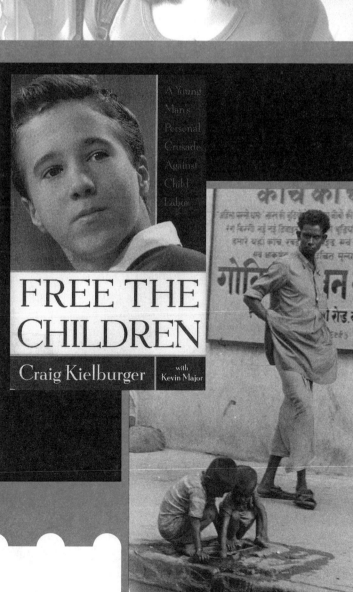

A Young Man's Personal Crusade Against Child Labor

FREE THE CHILDREN

Craig Kielburger with Kevin Major

Writers often have a purpose in mind. Sometimes the author's purpose is to persuade or entertain. Other times his or her purpose is to teach a lesson or tell some interesting truth. Knowing the author's purpose helps you understand and also judge whether the writing met the purpose.

BEFORE YOU READ

Look at the Anticipation Guide below.
1. Decide which of the statements are true and which are false.
2. After you finish reading the selection, return to each statement. Once again, decide which are true and which are false.

ANTICIPATION GUIDE

DIRECTIONS: Read these statements about life in the late 19th century. Mark statements that are true with a "T" and statements that are false with an "F."

BEFORE READING | AFTER READING

1. BEFORE 1900, THERE WERE NO SCHOOLS FOR THE BLIND.

2. PEOPLE WHO WERE DEAF DURING THE LATE 1800S HAD NO WAY OF COMMUNICATING.

3. HELEN KELLER LEARNED TO SPEAK, EVEN THOUGH SHE WAS DEAF.

4. BECAUSE OF HER DISABILITIES, COLLEGE WAS OUT OF THE QUESTION FOR HELEN.

5. HELEN BECAME A ROLE MODEL FOR PEOPLE AROUND THE WORLD.

READ
Read "Her Life Was Not a Joke."
1. Underline information that supports or contradicts the 5 statements.
2. Put a star next to anything that surprises you.
Note your **questions**.

"Her Life Was Not a Joke" by Bob Greene

I heard a comedian tell yet another Helen Keller joke the other night. He got the expected laugh; the comics usually do. When he mentioned Helen Keller's name, he rolled his eyes up into their sockets and flailed his arms about in a spastic motion.

That's how the jokes usually go. Helen Keller, in death, has become an easy target for dim-witted comics on cable stand-up shows and for kids who don't yet know they're being cruel. In our supposedly enlightened era, jokes about disabled people in general are frowned upon, but jokes about Helen Keller get told all the time. Sometimes it seems that this is destined to be Helen Keller's legacy—to be a punch line.

She doesn't need defending; she's been dead for more than twenty-five years now, and no one can hurt her feelings. But the staying power of Helen Keller jokes is more than just another depressing testament to the rampant stupidity of our know-nothing age; it is an insult to one of the most remarkable people who ever lived. Helen Keller was and is a hero to me, and her memory deserves better.

VOCABULARY
Helen Keller—mute, deaf, and blind woman (1880–1968) who rose above her disabilities
to help other disabled people to live fuller lives.
sockets—hollow parts into which the eyes fit.
flailed—waved or swung vigorously.
spastic—energetic; uncontrolled.
enlightened—intelligent and caring; without senseless cruelty.
rampant—widespread.

RESPONSE NOTES

EXAMPLE:
I haven't heard many! When was this written?

Helen Keller

How will Greene explain that Helen Keller's life is a serious matter? Greene would explain Helen Keller's life by saying how good of a person she was, and all that she accomplished

So at the risk of driving readers away—doubt that there's much of an audience for a biography of a woman people no longer care about—I'd like to explain who she was.

Helen Keller was born on June 27, 1880, in the Alabama town of Tuscumbia. A serious illness when she was nineteen months old took away her sight and hearing. She could not speak either; the world as we know it was lost to her. Or so it was assumed.

For the next five years, she grew up seeing nothing, hearing nothing, making only <u>guttural</u> sounds. Helen's father, in desperation, sought the advice of Dr. Alexander Graham Bell. Bell referred the Keller family to the Perkins Institution for the Blind in Boston. Through the Perkins Institution, Anne Mansfield Sullivan was sent to Alabama to try to free Helen from her self-contained prison.

Sullivan, twenty years old, had been blind herself, but had been <u>partially</u> cured. She arrived at the Kellers' home just before Helen's seventh birthday. Within one month she had begun to teach Helen the <u>manual</u> alphabet by spelling out words on her hand. Helen quickly learned the names of objects.

VOCABULARY
guttural—harsh; throaty.
partially—not completely.
manual—by hand.

"Her Life Was Not a Joke" continued

Helen learned to read Braille, and to write using a specially designed typewriter. At the Horace Mann School for the Deaf in Boston, she, at the age of ten, learned to speak.

What are 3 things Greene tells you about Helen Keller?

1. Helen learned to read Braille.
2. Helen learned how to talk at the age of ten.
3.

Helen enrolled at the Cambridge (Massachusetts) School for Young Ladies; Anne Sullivan accompanied her to classes, and conveyed the lectures to her by touch. Helen passed the entrance exams for Radcliffe College, one of the nation's most prestigious. There, too,

Helen Keller and Anne Sullivan

Sullivan went to classes with her to help her understand the lectures. In 1904 Helen graduated from Radcliffe with honors.

After graduation Helen devoted herself to the causes of blind and deaf people. With Sullivan's help, she wrote the classic autobiography *The Story of My Life*.

It was the first of many books she was to write, including *Optimism*, *The World I Live In*, *The Song of the Stone Wall*, *My Religion*, and *Teacher*. Her books were translated into more than fifty languages.

VOCABULARY
Braille—system of writing and printing for blind people.
conveyed the lectures—told her what her teachers said in classes.
prestigious—respected and important.

Her high-pitched voice was not easily understood, but she toured the world as a distinguished lecturer, advocating the rights of the disabled. Anne Sullivan, whose own blindness had recurred, died in 1936. Helen continued to lecture and travel, helped by her secretary Polly Thompson. She was an ardent opponent of fascism prior to World War II, and worked with soldiers who were blinded after that war broke out. She spoke before legislatures and governments in more than twenty-five countries. Among her many awards was the Chevalier's ribbon of the French Legion of Honor.

She died in Westport, Connecticut, on June 1, 1968, at the age of eighty-seven. From an early childhood that had seemed destined to cage her forever inside a sightless and soundless despair, she had become one of the most admired people in the world.

REFLECT

What would you say are Helen Keller's 3 most important achievements?

1. ....

2. ....

3. ....

REFLECT

So pardon me if I have to object to the easy stand-up jokes, the relegation of her to a reeling, buffoonish presence on comedy stages. In these days especially, with so many people endlessly complaining that their birthright in society makes them "victims," with so many people telling the rest of society how

Helen Keller with Anne Sullivan

VOCABULARY
advocating—speaking in favor of.
ardent—having or showing strong feelings; vigorous.
fascism—system of government in which an all-powerful leader rules.
legislatures—law-makers, such as members of Congress.
buffoonish—ridiculous; like a clown.
birthright—quality of life into which people are born, such as health, material possessions, race, nationality, and so forth.

"Her Life Was Not a Joke" continued

"disadvantaged" they are, the life of Helen Keller is not a bad reminder of what one person with courage can overcome.

If only more people in this lazy, sloppy-thinking age of ours would show that courage and that intellect. To those who would continue to use her memory as a source of ridicule, the best suggestion may be that they compare their own goals and accomplishments with hers, and then evaluate their time on Earth so far. To borrow a phrase that is overused these days, but seems applicable here: Get a life.

CLARIFY CLARIFY CLARIFY CLARIFY

I think Bob Greene's purpose in writing this piece was to
(circle all that apply):

ENTERTAIN

TEACH

REVEAL AN
IMPORTANT TRUTH

PERSUADE

How did "Her Life Was Not a Joke" make you feel about Helen Keller?

....

....

....

....

....

Photo of Helen Keller as a young woman

A. REFLECT What have you learned from the selection?

1. Return to the Anticipation Guide on page 124. Decide which statements are true and which are false.

2. Then explain what you learned about making easy jokes about other people.

What I Learned

_____

....

....

....

B. ORGANIZE WHAT YOU KNOW Bob Greene wants his readers to get to know the "real" Helen Keller. Has he met his purpose? Use the organizer below to organize what you know about Helen Keller.

GRAPHIC ORGANIZER

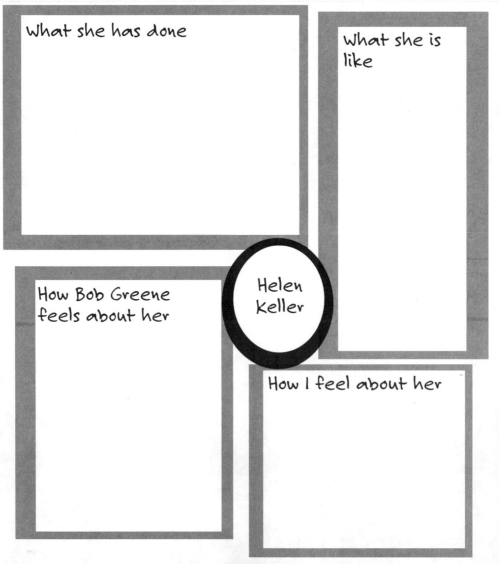

What she has done

What she is like

How Bob Greene feels about her

Helen Keller

How I feel about her

C. PLAN Now imagine you've been asked to write a "Get to Know_____" article for your school newspaper.

1. Start to plan your character sketch by deciding who you would like to write about. It can be a real or a fictional person.

2. Then fill in the graphic organizer below. Offer as much information about your person as you can.

What _____
has done

What _____
is like

Person's name:
_____

How others feel
about _____

How I feel
about _____

IV. WRITE

Use the information on your graphic organizer to help you write a **character sketch** about your person.

1. Start with a topic sentence that tells how you feel about your character.

2. Use the Writers' Checklist to help you revise.

WRAP-UP

What, in your own words, is Bob Greene's message for readers?

Helen Keller and Anne Sullivan

What have you done or accomplished in your life? What interesting things have happened to you? Everybody has a story to tell. Writers prove this everyday when they write about themselves.

BEFORE YOU READ

Get together with a partner.

1. Read the sentences from the autobiography "One Morning."

2. Put a 1 before the sentence that comes first in the excerpt, a 2 before the sentence that comes next, and so on. Share your answers.

3. Then answer the questions below.

_____ "Why was nothing being done to stop such cruelty?"

_____ "By the age of 12, he was free and travelling the world in his crusade against the horrors of child labor."

_____ "'Hi, Mom. The paper arrived yet?' I said, pouring cereal into a bowl."

_____ "Surely slavery had been abolished throughout the world by now."

I. What do you think "One Morning" is about?

....
....
....
....
....

2. How do you think you will like this story? Explain.

....
....
....
....
....

THINK–PAIR–SHARE

II. READ

Read "One Morning."

1. As you read, circle important events and sketch key scenes to help you **visualize** what you're reading.

2. Use the Graphic Organizer at the end to track the sequence of events in this excerpt from Kielburger's autobiography.

"One Morning" from *Free the Children* by Craig Kielburger

My mind goes back to April 19, 1995. I woke to sun streaming through my window, a welcome sign that summer was on its way. It was Wednesday, another school day, one I was looking forward to, in fact. Today were the tryouts for the cross-country running team.

As I stretched my way from under the blankets, I watched my dog go through her own waking-up ritual at the foot of my bed. I hauled on a pair of jeans and a sweatshirt.

"Hey, Muffin. Let's go, girl." I gave her a playful rub about her neck and off she went, racing ahead of me and down the stairs.

My mother, up for an hour or more already, was in the kitchen making lunches. The Kielburger household would soon be heading off to school. Both my parents are teachers. There were just the three of us; my older brother, Marc, had gone away to a junior college in January.

"Hi, Mom. The paper arrived yet?" I said, pouring cereal into a bowl.

"It's on the chair."

Every morning I read the comics before heading off to school. <u>Doonesbury</u>, <u>Calvin and Hobbes</u>, <u>Wizard of Id</u>. These are my favorites. If I find one particularly funny, sometimes I'll cut it out and post it on my

RESPONSE NOTES

EXAMPLE:

VOCABULARY

Doonesbury, Calvin and Hobbes, Wizard of Id—popular cartoons that appear in newspapers.

bulletin board, or tape it to one of my school books. We all can use a good laugh every day.

I picked up the *Toronto Star* and put it on the table. But I didn't make it past the front page. Staring back at me was the headline "BATTLED CHILD LABOR, BOY, 12, MURDERED." It was a jolt. Twelve, the same age as I was. My eyes fixed on the picture of a boy in a bright-red vest. He had a broad smile, his arm raised straight in the air, a fist clenched.

STOP AND THINK

Write 2 things the author has told you so far.

1.

2.

I read on. "Defied members of 'carpet mafia.'" Scenes from old movies came to my mind. But this wasn't any such mafia; the dateline was Pakistan. The boy was someone named Iqbal Masih.

I read quickly through the article, hardly believing the words before me.

ISLAMABAD, Pakistan (AP) - When Iqbal Masih was 4 years old, his parents sold him into slavery for less than $16.

For the next six years, he remained shackled to a carpet-weaving loom most of the time, tying tiny knots hour after hour.

By the age of 12, he was free and travelling the world in his crusade against the horrors of child labor.

VOCABULARY
mafia—a tightly organized criminal organization.
Pakistan—country in South Asia.
loom—tool for making thread or yarn into cloth.

"One Morning" continued

On Sunday, Iqbal was shot dead while he and two friends were riding their bikes in their village of Muridke, 35 kilometers outside the eastern city of Lahore. Some believe his murder was carried out by angry members of the carpet industry who had made repeated threats to silence the young activist.

STOP AND THINK

What 3 things happened to Iqbal Masih?

1.

2.

3.

I turned to my mother. "Have you read this? What exactly is child labor? Do you think he was really killed for standing up to this 'carpet mafia,' whatever that is?"

She was as lost for answers as I was. "Try the library at school," she suggested. "Maybe you'll find some information there."

Riding the bus to school later that morning, I could think of nothing but the article I had read on the front page. What kind of parents would sell their child into slavery at four years of age? And who would ever chain a child to a carpet loom?

Throughout the day I was consumed by Iqbal's story. In my Grade Seven class we had studied the American Civil War, and Abraham Lincoln, and how some of the slaves in the United States had escaped into Canada. But that was history from centuries ago. Surely slavery had been abolished throughout the world by now. If it wasn't, why had I never heard about it?

The school library was no help. After a thorough search I still hadn't found a scrap of information. After school, I decided to make the trek to the public library.

The librarian knew me from my previous visits. Luckily, she had read the same article that morning and was just as <u>intrigued</u>. Together, we searched out more information on child labor. We found a few newspaper and magazine articles, and made copies.

STOP AND THINK

What did Craig Keilburger do after reading Iqbal's story?

1.

2.

By the time I returned home, images of child labor had <u>imbedded</u> themselves in my mind: children younger than me forced to make carpets for endless hours in dimly lit rooms; others toiling in underground pits, struggling to get coal to the surface; others maimed or killed by explosions raging through fireworks factories. I was angry at the

VOCABULARY
intrigued—interested; curious.
imbedded—implanted; firmly established.

"One Morning" continued

world for letting these things happen to children. Why was nothing being done to stop such cruelty?

As I walked through my middle-class neighborhood, my thoughts were on the other side of the world. And my own world seemed a shade darker.

GRAPHIC ORGANIZER

WHO?

READ WHAT?

HOW DID IT AFFECT HIM?

WHAT DID HE DO?

IN THE END, HOW DID HE FEEL?

III. GATHER YOUR THOUGHTS

A. RETELL Return to the Graphic Organizer.

1. Then retell "One Morning" to a partner.

2. Next, ask your partner to retell the story to you.

3. Compare how your retellings were alike and different.

B. FIND A TOPIC Think of an event or a story that has to do with injustice.

1. If necessary, look in a magazine, scan the headlines, or listen to the news.

2. Narrow the topic in the spaces below.

EXAMPLE: Injustice

GENERAL SUBJECT	GENERAL SUBJECT

Slavery

ONE KIND OF INJUSTICE	ONE KIND OF INJUSTICE

Child slavery

SPECIFIC KIND OF INJUSTICE	SPECIFIC KIND OF INJUSTICE

C. RESEARCH AND ORGANIZE Research your subject.

1. Find books, articles, or use the Internet to search for more information.

2. Use the organizer below to help you organize facts that you can use to write an article.

1. What's the injustice?

2. What are the key facts?

3. How can the problem be solved or improved?

4. What's being done now?

IV. WRITE

Write an **article** to tell people about the injustice you have researched.

1. Refer to the organizer on the previous page to help you arrange your ideas.

2. Use the Writers' Checklist to help you revise.

Title:

Continue your writing on the next page.

WRITERS' CHECKLIST

APOSTROPHES

☐ Did you use apostrophes correctly to show possession? Possessive nouns show ownership. They are formed with an apostrophe (') and the letter *s* or an apostrophe alone. Add 's to most singular nouns. EXAMPLES: *Emma's* CD, *Mrs. Thomas's* book Add only an apostrophe to plural nouns that end in *s*. EXAMPLE: *the bees' hive* Add 's to plural nouns that do not end in *s*. EXAMPLE: *The children's lunch*

☐ Did you use apostrophes correctly in contractions? Apostrophes are also used with contractions to show that a word has been shortened. EXAMPLES: *cannot—can't, do not—don't, it is—it's*

Continue your writing from the previous page.

V. WRAP-UP

How did "One Morning" make you feel? Explain.

Knights and Chivalry

Chivalry was an important part of a knight's life. It meant being brave, courteous, and gentlemanly.

The Feudal System

King or Queen

Nobles and Knights

Church

Servants

The feudal system thrived during the Middle Ages (1000–1300). It was a time when kings ruled absolutely, and knights fought in battles to prove their courage and loyalty.

Good readers prepare before they begin. They look over a selection and think to themselves, "What do I already know about this topic? What questions do I have about it?" Asking such questions before you read helps you organize your thoughts.

BEFORE YOU READ

I.

Read the title and first paragraph.
1. Think about what you already know about this topic.
2. Use the K-W-L Chart on the next page.

"The Knight in Person" by Julek Heller

The medieval knight was probably not far removed in physique from his twentieth-century counterpart. He was perhaps a little shorter, with broad shoulders and strong arms, and undoubtedly robust, for not only did he take a great deal of physical exercise but also he had survived his medieval childhood, with its constant threat of diseases such as typhus, cholera, smallpox and infection from wounds, polluted water and vermin.

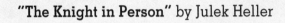

VOCABULARY

medieval—from the Middle Ages.
physique—shape and appearance.
counterpart—person or thing that is exactly, or very much like, another.
robust—full of health and energy.
typhus, cholera, smallpox—easily communicated diseases.
vermin—small animals or insects, such as rats and cockroaches.

K-W-L Chart

✣✣✣✣✣✣✣✣✣✣✣✣✣✣✣✣✣✣✣✣✣✣✣✣✣✣✣

K
Write what you already know about the topic of the selection—knights.

WHAT I **K**NOW

✣✣✣✣✣✣✣✣✣✣✣✣✣✣✣✣✣✣✣✣✣✣✣✣✣✣✣

W
Think about and list what you want to know about knights.

WHAT I **W**ANT TO KNOW

✣✣✣✣✣✣✣✣✣✣✣✣✣✣✣✣✣✣✣✣✣✣✣✣✣✣✣

L
After you read, record what you learned in answering your questions.

WHAT I **L**EARNED

READ

Read through the selection at your own pace.

1. As you read, keep in mind your questions in the K-W-L Chart.

2. Mark or **highlight** parts of the article that answer your questions.

Response Notes

EXAMPLE:
They died
young!

"The Knight in Person" continued

The close proximity of death (the average life-expectancy for those who survived to adulthood was only thirty to thirty-five years) certainly made men more superstitious. Knights believed implicitly in omens and predictions and tried to protect themselves by wearing religious medallions and carrying holy relics on their journeys.

stop+think

Why were knights superstitious?

....

....

....

stop+think

Blindness, caused by disease, was far more common than it is today, but this was seemingly no major hindrance, as the blind King of Bohemia tried to show when he rode into battle on his horse led by two knights. Not surprisingly, the king was killed in the battle.

Knights were very vain about their appearance, but it was their own opinion of their appearance which counted more than reality. One knight ravaged a neighbor's land after receiving what he considered to

VOCABULARY

proximity—nearness.
life-expectancy—length of life.
superstitious—believing that something unrelated to an event influences its outcome.
omens—signs of good or bad events to come.
medallions—round ornaments, often displaying a saint's picture.
holy relics—objects kept for their association with things sacred and religious.
hindrance—something that stands in the way; obstacle.
ravaged—destroyed violently.

"The Knight in Person" continued

be a <u>slur</u> against his looks. In fact, knights bore the marks of their lifestyle: scars, scratches, slit noses, missing ears and teeth—<u>legacies</u> of a lifetime of fighting.

But knights took some care with their looks. Some knights, no doubt well-groomed, were even chosen as 'pin-ups', as spinning songs sung by women during the <u>Crusades</u> reveal. They would permit their hair to be combed, washed and oiled. Some even had their hair curled with hot <u>tongs</u>, and they were not above having their hair <u>hennaed</u> to improve its <u>luster</u>. However, it was no pleasure for a knight to have his hair cut because scissors at this time were rather like crude garden <u>shears</u> which did not cut cleanly.

stop+think

How did the knights feel about how they looked?

_____

_____

_____

Many contemporary pictures show clean-shaven knights. Shaving must have been an uncomfortable procedure, for razors then resembled giant carving knives and there was no hot water or soap. But beards did have their vogue, and in twelfth-century France there was a fashion for wearing small, tufted beards into which knights wove little strands of gold thread.

VOCABULARY
slur—insult.
legacies—marks of the past.
Crusades—wars undertaken by European Christians in the 11th, 12th, and 13th centuries to recover the Holy Land from the Muslims.
tongs—grasping device made up of two arms joined at one end.
hennaed—colored or dyed.
luster—brightness.
shears—scissors.

"The Knight in Person' continued

Contrary to popular belief knights took baths frequently. It was often the only way to relax after many hours in the saddle wearing armor, or to ease the bruises and grazes received in fights. It also eased the discomfort from flea-bites, which were part and parcel of living in a castle. When visitors arrived at a castle they would immediately be offered a bath and a change of clothes. The medieval bath resembled a wooden tub with a seat in it, on which the knight would sit while hot, perfumed or oiled water was poured round him. It was not uncommon for young women to attend the knight in his bath.

Knights were not so particular about their clothing, which was washed very infrequently—if at all. However, at the end of the day when he retired to bed, the knight would discard all his clothing. Some medieval pictures show us kings in bed wearing their crowns and nothing else.

VOCABULARY

armor—heavy metal worn to protect the body in battle.
part and parcel—basic or essential parts.
infrequently—not often.
retired—got ready to sleep.

stop+think

What did knights do to take care of their physical appearance?

What does their concern about their looks tell you about knights?

GATHER YOUR THOUGHTS

A. REFLECT Now go back to your K-W-L Chart on page 145.

1. In the **L** space, write the answers to your questions about knights. You may not be able to answer all the questions, but don't worry. Answer the ones you can.

2. If you came up with new questions, add them to the chart.

B. FIND THE MAIN IDEAS Plan a summary of the article. Sort out the most important ideas from the smaller ones. A summary does not include the small details. Use the chart to help you.

MAIN IDEAS

DETAILS

DETAILS

DETAILS

DETAILS

C. WRITE A TOPIC SENTENCE Fill in the blanks to create your topic sentence. Tell the most important idea of the selection.

"The Knight in Person" is an article about _____

that describes _____.

IV. WRITE

Develop your ideas into a **summary** of the most important ideas of the selection. Write so that someone who has not read the selection can understand what it is about.

1. Begin with the topic sentence you developed on the previous page.
2. Cover the ideas in the order they appear in the article.
3. Use the Writers' Checklist to help you revise.

V. WRAP-UP

What made the selection easy or hard for you to read?

The Victorious Feudal Knight

Coming attractions at the movies are used to persuade you to see the whole movie. They introduce you to the main characters and to the most important parts of the story. They help you become familiar with a movie even before you've seen it. A preview can do the same thing for you in reading.

 BEFORE YOU READ
Good readers preview before they read. They look at illustrations and read any titles, captions, and headings that appear. Preview "The Victorious Feudal Knight."

Knight on horseback during a battle

Preview

1. Start with the title. What do the words mean? Use a dictionary if you need to.

"Victorious Feudal Knight" means

2. Look at the illustrations and read the captions.
What do the illustrations and captions tell you about feudal knights?

3. Use your preview and knowledge of knights to prepare you for reading.

MAKE A PREDICTION

SET PURPOSES

I predict this selection will . . .

As I read, I want to find out . . .

II. READ

As you read, think about the information being given.

1. Circle words or phrases that tell you about knights and the feudal system.
2. Put your **reactions** to these subjects in the Response Notes.

Response Notes

"The Victorious Feudal Knight" by Jay Williams

Duke William—now <u>King William the Conqueror</u>—was the master of a rich land, but an uneasy one. For the next five years he faced one uprising after another from stubborn and independent <u>Saxon</u> lords. When the rebels were at last put down, all the lands of England were owned by the <u>Crown</u>. William set about imposing his government on the country and giving rich estates to the adventurers who had followed his <u>banners</u> against King Harold. To those who cooperated with him he held out the prospect of great power and wealth; in return he received from them the pledge of military service and of personal loyalty. By doing so, he was bringing England into the unique pattern of life that made the <u>Crusades</u> desirable and possible.

EXAMPLE:
Each side gets something in the deal!

VOCABULARY

King William the Conqueror—King of England from 1066–87 who led the Norman invasion of England to win the Battle of Hastings.
Saxon—English or Scottish.
Crown—the king; monarchy.
estates—large pieces of land in the country.
banners—flags of a nation marking allegiance to the king.
Crusades—wars undertaken by the European Christians in the 11th, 12th, and 13th centuries to recover the Holy Land from the Muslims.

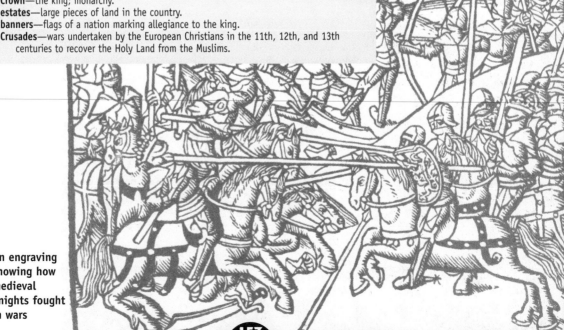

An engraving showing how medieval knights fought in wars

The new pattern that the Normans brought into England is now called the feudal system. Under <u>feudalism</u>, only the king owned land—and even he, it was recognized, held his land from God. All other men were <u>tenants</u>. A man was lord of a region which he held from another man, and ultimately from the king, in exchange for the performance of a certain service, called a fee. This tight-knit relationship between a lord and his tenant, or <u>vassal</u>, had already spread over most of Europe; and now England was also bound in feudalism. Before many years, that feudal relationship, based on service, would find itself transported far across the sea to the <u>Holy Land</u>.

For <u>warriors</u>, feudalism meant military duty. When his lord called him, the mounted rider had to appear with his men, fully armed and ready to fight, for forty days in each year. In addition, he gave money when it was needed for special purposes, and he had to attend his lord's court and give advice or sit in judgment. If he failed in his fee, he <u>forfeited</u> his land. His children could only inherit the estate after him if they made a payment and agreed to the same conditions that their father had fulfilled.

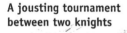

A jousting tournament between two knights

V O C A B U L A R Y

feudalism—political and economic system of Europe in the Middle Ages.
tenants—people who pay rent to live on or use property that is owned by another person.
vassal—person who was granted protection, land, or the use of land in return for loyal support and military service to the lord.
Holy Land—the Biblical region of Palestine.
warriors—people who are involved in war and fighting.
forfeited—lost or gave up because of a fault, error, or offense.

What did you find out about feudalism? Use this graphic organizer to arrange what you learned so far.

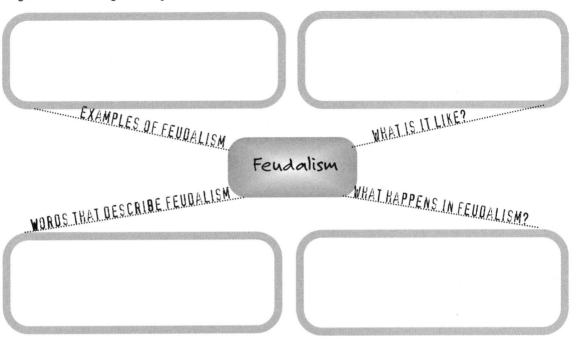

EXAMPLES OF FEUDALISM

WHAT IS IT LIKE?

Feudalism

WORDS THAT DESCRIBE FEUDALISM

WHAT HAPPENS IN FEUDALISM?

"The Victorious Feudal Knight" continued

The mailed cavalry of Europe, the riders who had destroyed King Harold's shield-wall, called themselves *chevaliers*, or horsemen. The English had a word for the free fighting men who followed a nobleman: the word *cniht*, or as it was later spelled, knight. This word came to mean the special class of armed and mounted landholders. There were other mounted men-at-arms called *serviens*, or sergeants; we may think of them as a grade below the knights, not quite so noble, not always giving military service as their fee. Both knight and sergeant were warriors. We must not imagine them to be clean-shaven, curly-headed Galahads or gentle, bright-eyed, medieval Boy Scouts, as they usually appear in romantic paintings or motion pictures. War was their trade, their livelihood, and they were generally good for nothing else.

V O C A B U L A R Y
mailed—covered with protective armor.
cavalry—troops trained to fight on horseback.
nobleman—man of high rank and social status.
Galahads—noble, pure, and heroic people; refers to the Arthurian legend of Sir Galahad, a knight who succeeded in his quest to find the Holy Grail.

The knights of the eleventh century were trained from childhood in the use of arms. They were taught to shoot the clumsy shortbow, to ride and wrestle, and to handle the <u>lance</u>, the sword, the long-hafted axe, and the <u>mace</u>. Training in horsemanship was vital. The knight's horse had to be taught to turn, to <u>canter,</u> to halt without the touch of the <u>reins</u>, and to stand still if its master was unseated so that he could remount. The young soldier had to wear his <u>armor</u> until he thought nothing of its dragging weight. A <u>shirt of mail</u> might weigh from twenty to thirty pounds, plus the additional weight of a padded coat, called a *gambeson*, worn under the mail. Then, there was his steel and leather helmet and his kite-shaped shield, which together added perhaps another six or seven pounds. Furthermore, he wore a belt, a <u>scabbard</u>, a sword, and a <u>dagger</u>, and carried a lance and maybe an axe, so that all in all he might be lugging more than a third of his own weight into battle. It comes as something of a shock to think what sheer hard work it must have been to fight in armor.

We can think of the knight of this period as a soldier who owned a farm that was also his fort. This soldier-farmer became a knight because his lord made him one. The only ritual involved might be that his lord struck him on the shoulder, saying, "Be worthy. I make you a knight."

A knight kneeling before his lord

VOCABULARY
lance—weapon like a spear.
mace—clublike weapon.
canter—gallop slowly.
reins—long leather straps held by the rider to control a horse.
armor—heavy covering, especially of metal, worn to protect the body in battle.
shirt of mail—heavy metal shirt worn for protection.
scabbard—case for the blade of a sword or knife.
dagger—short, pointed weapon like a knife.

"**The Victorious Feudal Knight**" continued

Knights relied upon their swords to make their way in the world, and many were consequently little better than robbers. The records are full of complaints against these mailed "devils and scoundrels."

There were, however, virtues that distinguished a knight from other men. These were simple enough, and they grew naturally out of the feudal system: courage, loyalty, and service were demanded of one who wore the armor, sword-belt, and spurs of the *chevalier*.

Without courage a man was useless in battle. Without loyalty the whole structure of the oath of fealty and the giving of homage would have fallen apart. Men had to keep their oaths and remain true to their lords. Moreover, savage as that age was, it was deeply religious, pervaded by the spirit of the Christian Church.

VOCABULARY
scoundrels—wicked people.
fealty—duty; loyalty.
homage—special public honor or respect.
pervaded—marked everywhere.

Knights

WHAT THEY LOOKED LIKE

WHAT THEY DID

WHAT THEY WERE LIKE

A. CHOOSE A TOPIC Use details from the selection to choose a topic on feudalism that you can write about.

My paragraph will explain . . .

....

....

....

Use the web below to brainstorm some important words or facts about your topic. Write your topic in the center circle.

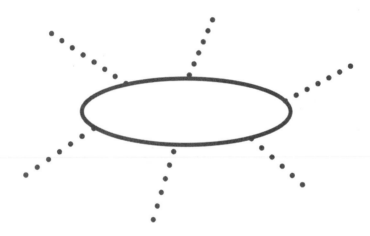

B. DEVELOP A TOPIC SENTENCE Now write a topic sentence for an expository paragraph. It should tell readers what the paragraph will be about and state the main point about your topic.

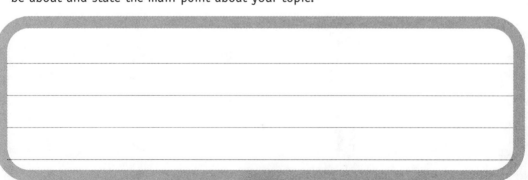

IV. WRITE

Write an **expository paragraph** about your topic.

1. Remember to start with your topic sentence.

2. Use the Writers' Checklist to help you revise.

WRITERS' CHECKLIST

COMMAS

Dependent clauses should not stand alone as sentences. When they are part of a sentence, they often need to be set off by commas.

☐ Did you use commas to set off introductory dependent clauses?

EXAMPLE: Although artists often paint knights as gentle, knights were warriors who often did nothing but fight.

☐ Did you use commas to set off dependent clauses within a sentence? EXAMPLE: A knight, before he could go into battle, had to learn how to support equipment that was one third of his own weight.

Explain whether or not you would recommend "The Victorious Feudal Knight" to someone.

A 19th century engraving of a medieval knight in full battle armor

Sir Sagramor le Desirous

Naguib Mahfouz

Naguib Mahfouz (1911–) was born in Egypt, the youngest of seven children. One of Egypt's most famous writers, he has written novels, short stories, and screenplays for films.

ECHOES OF AN AUTOBIOGRAPHY

FOREWORD BY NADINE GORDIMER

NAGUIB MAHFOUZ

WINNER OF THE NOBEL PRIZE FOR LITERATURE

Egypt

Africa

17: **Forgetfulness** and **An Unwritten Letter**

There are advantages to listening to a story read aloud. One is that the reader can use tone of voice, facial expressions, and hand movements to help you understand the selection.

I. BEFORE YOU READ

Get together with a partner or small group.
1. Decide who will read first.
2. Then read aloud the memoir on page 163, switching readers about halfway through.
3. Complete the Listener's Guide below.
4. Compare responses with your partner. Discuss how they were alike and how they were different.

LISTENER'S GUIDE

AUTHOR:

TITLE:

WORDS I REMEMBERED:

WHAT I THINK ABOUT IT:

II. READ

Now read "Forgetfulness" and "An Unwritten Letter" to yourself.

1. Circle or underline sights and sounds that catch your attention.

2. As you read, write your **questions** in the Response Notes.

"Forgetfulness" from *Echoes of an Autobiography* by Naguib Mahfouz

RESPONSE NOTES

Who is this old man who leaves his home each morning to walk about, getting as much exercise as he can?

He is the <u>sheikh</u>, the teacher of Arabic, who was retired more than twenty years ago.

Whenever he feels tired he sits down on the <u>pavement</u>, or on the stone wall of the garden of a house, leaning on his stick and drying his sweat <u>with the end of his flowing <u>gallabiya</u></u>. The <u>quarter</u> knows him and the people love him; but seldom does anyone greet him, because of his weak memory and senses. He has forgotten relatives and neighbors, students and the rules of grammar.

EXAMPLE:

Is he sad— or in pain?

▰ VOCABULARY ▰

sheikh—male leader of an Arab family or village.
pavement—paved surface or road.
gallabiya—robe.
quarter—section of a city.

READER'S LOG

Write what you think this sentence from the story means.

"He has forgotten relatives and neighbors, students and the rules of grammar."

"An Unwritten Letter" from *Echoes of an Autobiography*
by Naguib Mahfouz

In the same year I learned of Hammam's appointment as head of the court of appeals of Alexandria and read the news of the <u>execution</u> of Sayyid al-Ghadban for murdering a dancer. The three of us—Hammam, al-Ghadban, and I—had been childhood friends. Al-Ghadban had been the center of attention because of his beautiful voice and <u>scabrous</u> anecdotes. We had parted before reaching the age of nine and each had gone his separate way. I learned from some relatives that Hammam had gone into the <u>judiciary</u>, while I followed the news of al-Ghadban in the artistic press as a bouncer in a nightclub.

READER'S LOG

Write about how this sentence makes you feel. Then choose another phrase or sentence from the memoir. Copy it below and then write your thoughts about it.

"The three of us—Hammam, al-Ghadban, and I—had been childhood friends."

VOCABULARY
execution—putting to death.
scabrous—scandalous or bad.
judiciary—system of courts of law for the government.

"An Unwritten Letter" CONTINUED

In truth, the news of his execution shook me and carried me off to reflecting on times past. I thought of writing a letter to Hammam expressing my feelings and thoughts. I began writing it, but then stopped, for my enthusiasm had <u>waned</u>, thinking that he would have forgotten those times and those people, or that he was no longer concerned about such emotions.

VOCABULARY
waned—become gradually less.

RESPONSE NOTES

READER'S LOG

Write about how this sentence from the memoir makes you feel. Then choose another sentence, copy it below, and write your thoughts about it.

"I thought of writing a letter to Hammam expressing my feelings and thoughts. I began writing it, but then stopped, for my enthusiasm had waned . . ."

GATHER YOUR THOUGHTS

A. BRAINSTORM Some of the people Mahfouz writes about seem lonely. Everyone has his or her own ideas about what loneliness looks and sounds like. With a partner or small group, do some brainstorming. What are the sights or sounds that can make a person feel alone?

1. Share your ideas with others in the class.

2. Record the sights and sounds below.

SIGHTS AND SOUNDS OF LONELINESS

EXAMPLE:	EXAMPLE:
sight of a tree with no leaves	sound of train whistle

B. REMEMBER EXPERIENCES Prepare to write an anecdote (a short, interesting account) of a time you felt lonely.

1. List several times when you felt lonely.

2. Take a few minutes to look over your list. Put a check mark (✔) by the experience that would make for an interesting anecdote.

C. FOCUS ON A TOPIC Help yourself get ready to write an anecdote by making some notes about the experience.
1. Focus on one moment.
2. Then answer each question below.

When was it?

....

....

Where were you?

....

....

What happened?

....

....

What were you thinking and feeling?

....

....

Was anyone else involved?

....

....

D. USE SENSORY LANGUAGE Make your writing come alive by using sensory language—words that appeal to one or more of the five senses: sight, sound, smell, taste, and touch.
1. Fill the spokes of the web below with sensory words about your experience. Use images from the chart as appropriate.
2. Add more spokes as necessary.

When
I felt alone

WRITE

Write an **anecdote**, a short paragraph describing your experience of loneliness.

1. Write in the first person (*I said*, *we felt*, and so on).
2. Add sensory language from your web to make your description more vivid.
3. Use the Writers' Checklist to help you revise.

WRITERS' CHECKLIST
ADJECTIVES and ADVERBS

Descriptive writing often contains many adjectives and adverbs. Use them carefully.

❑ Did you use adverbs, not adjectives, to describe verbs?
EXAMPLE: *The trumpeter played the song softly.* (*not* soft)

❑ Did you use the correct (comparative) form to compare 2 things? EXAMPLE: *Of the two lakes, this one is cleaner.* (*not* more cleaner *or* the cleanest)

❑ Did you use the correct (superlative) form to compare 3 or more things? EXAMPLE: *The painting was the most beautiful of all in the whole museum.* (*not* more beautiful than all)

V. WRAP-UP

What were some parts of Naguib Mahfouz's writing style that you liked or found unusual?

_____

_____

_____

_____

_____

_____

_____

_____

_____

_____

READERS' CHECKLIST
STYLE

☐ Did you find the passage well written?

☐ Are the sentences well constructed and the words well chosen?

☐ Does the style show you how to be a better writer?

People learn best when they can "hook" new information onto what they already know. Calling to mind what you know about a topic will help you learn and remember what you read.

BEFORE YOU READ

I.

Sometimes a word or idea is very important to a piece of writing. Creating a web can often help you better understand that word or idea.

1. With a partner, use the web below to think about *justice*. It's a word that appears often in Mahfouz's writing.

2. List words, phrases, or situations that you associate with the idea of justice.

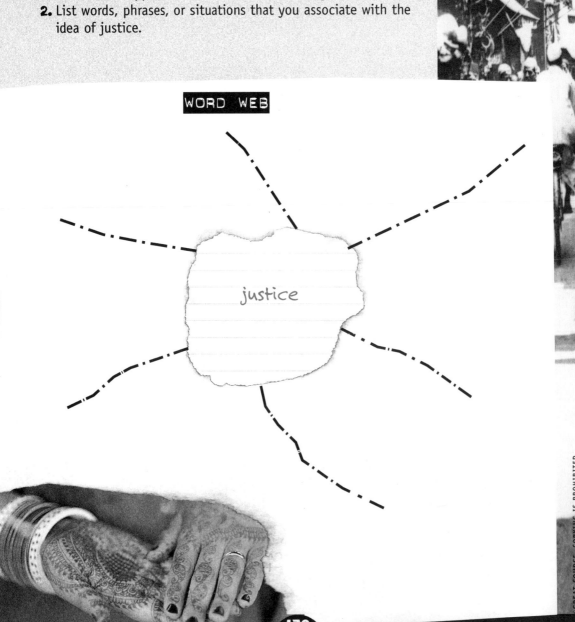

WORD WEB

justice

READ

Now read "A Man Reserves a Seat" and "Justice."
1. As you read, think about *justice*.
2. Help yourself **visualize** what Mahfouz is describing by making a sketch in the Response Notes.

"A Man Reserves a Seat" from *Echoes of an Autobiography* by Naguib Mahfouz

The bus started on its journey from <u>Zeytoun</u> at the same moment that a private car set forth from the owner's house in <u>Helwan</u>. Each varied the speed at which it was traveling, speeding along and then slowing down, and perhaps coming to a stop for a minute or more depending on the state of the traffic.

STOP AND PREDICT

What do you predict will happen to the bus and car?

They both, however, reached Station Square at the same time, and even had a slight accident, in which one of the bus's headlights was broken and the front of the car was scratched.

A man was passing and was crushed between the two vehicles and died. He was crossing the square in order to book a seat on the train going to <u>Upper Egypt</u>.

EXAMPLE:

VOCABULARY

Zeytoun—name of a town.
Helwan—also the name of a town.
Upper Egypt—the southern part of Egypt.

"Justice" from *Echoes of an Autobiography*
by Naguib Mahfouz

I went unhesitatingly to a well-known lawyer. How splendid was his frankness when he said to me, "You are in the right, but the opposing party is also in the right."

"I proposed to him," I said, "that we should seek the decision of some person in whom we both had confidence."

"There's no hope of finding such a person in this day and age!"

"I have registered letters which will convince the court of my honesty."

"They may be challenged as being forged."

"The fact is that I'm one hundred percent innocent."

"There's no one who is one hundred percent innocent."

STOP AND PREDICT

Do you think the person will be "one hundred percent innocent"? Explain why or why not.

_____

_____

_____

VOCABULARY
frankness—openness in expressing thoughts and feelings.
forged—copied in order to deceive or trick.

NAGUIB MAHFOUZ

"Justice" CONTINUED

"It's not impossible."

"Did you not, in a moment of anger, threaten to kill him?"

"He didn't take what I said seriously."

"But he took many precautions, paid visits to various shrines, and made solemn pledges."

I burst out laughing. "That was madness."

"It is up to you to prove he's mad, especially as his lawyer will on his part try to prove that it's you who are mad."

My peals of laughter were interrupted by the lawyer: "There's nothing to laugh about."

"To accuse me of madness is enough to make one laugh."

"Rather, it induces sorrow."

"And why is that, sir?"

"Madness induces sorrow."

STOP aND THiNK

Will the man who comes to the lawyer find the justice he is after? Explain why or why not.

VOCABULARY

precautions—actions taken to prevent possible danger or problems.
solemn pledges—promises that are made with great seriousness.
madness—craziness; unstable state of mind.
induces—brings about; causes.

©GREAT SOURCE. COPYING IS PROHIBITED.

RESPONSE NOTES

"Seeing that I'm in my right senses, the accusation is not relevant."

"But being concerned may in itself mean madness."

"Are you in any doubt about my state of mind?" I asked in <u>consternation</u>.

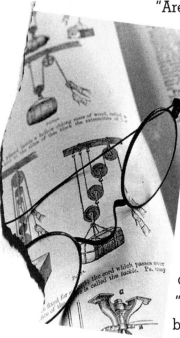

"Indeed, I am convinced—your <u>inveterate</u> disagreement indicates that you are *both* mad."

"And yet you showed yourself quite prepared to defend me?"

"It's my duty."

The lawyer gave a deep-seated sigh and continued. "And don't forget I'm as mad as both of you."

VOCABULARY
consternation—dismay; fear.
inveterate—persistent.

STOP AND REFLECT

Which of your predictions were right? Which ones were wrong? Why?

What parts of the text helped you predict?

GATHER YOUR THOUGHTS

A. REVIEW Reread "A Man Reserves a Seat." Use the plot chart below to show the sequence of events in the story.

THE PLOT OF "A MAN RESERVES A SEAT"

FIRST,

NEXT,

THEN,

FINALLY,

B. REFLECT Reflect on the author's message. Either alone or with a partner, answer these 2 questions.

1. What does "A Man Reserves a Seat" say about justice?

2. What does "Justice" say about justice?

C. PLAN Now plan your own story about justice.

1. Get some ideas by reviewing the web you made on page 170.

2. Then decide who will be in the story and where and when it will take place. Make some notes here.

Who?

Where?

When?

Idea you want to get across:

D. CREATE A STORYBOARD Create a plot chart similar to the one on page 175. Your chart can help you plan what will happen in your story.

THE PLOT OF MY STORY

FIRST,

NEXT,

THEN,

FINALLY,

IV. WRITE

Now write a **story** about justice. Refer to your plot chart as you write.
1. Remember to give your story a title.
2. Use the Writers' Checklist to help you revise.

WRITERS' CHECKLIST

SUBJECT–VERB AGREEMENT

❑ **Did you use singular verbs for singular subjects?**

❑ **Did you use plural verbs for plural subjects?**

The subject and verb of a sentence must work together, or agree. A sentence with a singular subject *(the man)* must have a singular verb *(walks)*. A sentence with a plural subject *(they)* must have a verb that works with a plural subject *(walk)*.

EXAMPLES:

correct: A *man walks* to the bus.

incorrect: They *walks* to the bus.

Continue your writing from the previous page.

WRAP-UP

What things did Naguib Mahfouz's stories make you think about?

Booker T. Washington

Discrimination

The end of slavery in America in 1865 meant African Americans had more rights, but many still faced harsh discrimination. Such inspirational figures as Booker T. Washington and Rosa Parks helped to lead the battle against the unfair treatment of black Americans.

Rosa Parks

HOTEL CLARK

The Best Service for COLORED ONLY
144

19: Ancestry

Do you know what it means to look ahead, or *anticipate*? When you anticipate rain, for example, you carry an umbrella. If you look at the title of a selection or how it is introduced, you can anticipate what the selection might be about.

BEFORE YOU READ

Use the Anticipation Guide to think ahead about the selection.
1. Read each of the statements below.
2. Mark whether you *agree* or *disagree* with each statement.

Anticipation Guide

BEFORE YOU READ			AFTER YOU READ	
agree	disagree		agree	disagree

1. MANY PEOPLE DON'T KNOW MUCH ABOUT THEIR ANCESTORS.

2. IT'S IMPORTANT FOR CHILDREN TO KNOW ABOUT THEIR ANCESTORS.

3. ONE'S NAME IS AN IMPORTANT PART OF ONE'S IDENTITY.

3. Discuss your answers with a partner. Did you agree or disagree? Why?
4. Think about the title "Ancestry." What clues does it give about the selection? Write several predictions below.

What I Expect:

1.

2.

3.

II. READ

Now read the selection at your own pace.
1. As you read, use the Response Notes space to **predict** what you think will happen.
2. Circle or underline information that relates to your predictions.

"Ancestry" from *Up from Slavery*
by Booker T. Washington

When, however, I found myself at the school for the first time, I also found myself <u>confronted</u> with two other difficulties. In the first place, I found that all of the other children wore hats or caps on their heads, and I had neither hat nor cap. In fact, I do not remember that up to the time of going to school I had ever worn any kind of covering upon my head, nor do I recall that either I or anybody else had even thought anything about the need of covering for my head. But, of course, when I saw how all the other boys were dressed, I began to feel quite uncomfortable. As usual, I put the case before my mother, and she explained to me that she had no money with which to buy a "store hat," which was a rather new institution at that time among the members of my race and was considered quite the thing for young and old to own, but that she would find a way to help me out of the difficulty. She accordingly got two pieces of "<u>homespun</u>" (jeans) and sewed them together, and I was soon the proud possessor of my first cap.

The lesson that my mother taught me in this has always remained with me, and I have tried as best I could to teach it to others. I have always felt proud, whenever I think of the incident, that my mother had strength of character enough not to be led into the temptation of seeming to be that which she was not—of trying to impress my schoolmates and others with the fact that she was able to buy me a "store hat "when

EXAMPLE:
He will be teased because of the hat.

VOCABULARY
confronted—come face to face with.
homespun—made of plain cloth; made by hand.

"Ancestry" continued

she was not. I have always felt proud that she refused to go into debt for that which she did not have the money to pay for. Since that time I have owned many kinds of caps and hats, but never one of which I have felt so proud as of the cap made of the two pieces of cloth sewed together by my mother. I have noted the fact, but without satisfaction, I need not add, that several of the boys who began their careers with "store hats" and who were my schoolmates and used to join in the sport that was made of me because I had only a "homespun" cap, have ended their careers in the penitentiary, while others are not able now to buy any kind of hat.

Yes, he was teased!

stop + retell

Retell in your own words what has happened so far. Think about these questions:

• Who is telling about the events?   • What has he described?

_____

_____

My second difficulty was with regard to my name, or rather a name. From the time when I could remember anything, I had been called simply "Booker." Before going to school it had never occurred to me that it was needful or appropriate to have an additional name. When I heard the school-roll called, I noticed that all of the children had at least two names, and some of them indulged in what seemed to me the extravagance of having three. I was in deep perplexity, because I knew that the teacher would demand of me at least two names, and I had only one. By the time the occasion came for the enrolling of my name, an idea occurred to me which I thought would make me equal to the situation; and so, when the teacher asked me

VOCABULARY
extravagance—luxury; unwise spending of money.
perplexity—confusion; uncertainty.

what my full name was, I calmly told him "Booker Washington," as if I had been called by that name all my life; and by that name I have since been known. Later in my life I found that my mother had given me the name of "Booker Taliaferro" soon after I was born, but in some way that part of my name seemed to disappear and for a long while was forgotten, but as soon as I found out about it I revived it, and made my full name "Booker Taliaferro Washington." I think there are not many men in our country who have had the <u>privilege</u> of naming themselves in the way that I have.

More than once I have tried to picture myself in the position of a boy or man with an honored and distinguished <u>ancestry</u> which I could trace back through a period of hundreds of years, and who had not only inherited a name, but fortune and a proud family <u>homestead</u>; and yet I have sometimes had the feeling that if I had <u>inherited</u> these, and had been a member of a more popular race, I should have been inclined to yield to the <u>temptation</u> of depending upon my ancestry and my color to do that for me which I should do for myself. Years ago I resolved that because I had no ancestry myself I would leave a record of which my children would be proud, and which might encourage them to still higher effort.

The world should not pass judgment upon the Negro, and especially the Negro youth, too quickly or too harshly. The Negro boy has <u>obstacles</u>, discouragements, and temptations to battle with that are little known to those not situated as he is. When a white boy undertakes a task, it is taken for granted that he will succeed. On the other hand, people are

VOCABULARY

privilege—special right or benefit that is granted to or enjoyed by some people and not others.
ancestry—people who make up a line of descent or heritage.
homestead—house with the land and buildings belonging to it.
inherited—received after someone's death.
temptation—something that is greatly appealing.
obstacles—things that block or stand in the way.

usually surprised if the Negro boy does not fail. In a word, the Negro youth starts out with the presumption against him.

The influence of ancestry, however, is important in helping forward any individual or race, if too much reliance is not placed upon it. Those who constantly direct attention to the Negro youth's moral weaknesses, and compare his advancement with that of white youths, do not consider the influence of the memories which cling about the old family homesteads. I have no idea, as I have stated elsewhere, who my grandmother was. I have, or have had, uncles and aunts and cousins, but I have no knowledge as to where most of them are. My case will illustrate that of hundreds of thousands of black people in every part of our country. The very fact that the white boy is conscious that, if he fails in life, he will disgrace the whole family record, extending back through many generations, is of tremendous value in helping him to resist temptations. The fact that the individual has behind and surrounding him proud family history and connection serves as a stimulus to help him to overcome obstacles when striving for success.

VOCABULARY
presumption—assumption; supposition.
reliance—dependence.
stimulus—motivation.

stop + retell

1. Now return to the Anticipation Guide on page 180. Mark how you feel about each statement. Discuss your answers with a partner.
2. Retell the rest of the selection.

GATHER YOUR THOUGHTS

A. SHAPE AN OPINION An *opinion* is a person's thought or belief. A *fact* is something that can be proven true or false.

Booker T. Washington gives his own opinions about the power of ancestry and a name. Shape your own opinion about what Washington says. Start with a general opinion:

(circle one)

One's ancestry   does   does not
have a strong influence on one's life.

B. SUPPORT YOUR OPINION Writers support their opinions with facts, examples and experiences, and statements by experts. In the chart below, write at least 3 forms of support for your opinion about ancestry.

OPINION STATEMENT

FACTS	EXAMPLES AND EXPERIENCES	WASHINGTON'S STATEMENTS

IV. WRITE

Now use your opinion to write a **persuasive paragraph**.

1. Support your opinion with facts, examples, and statements from the chart.

2. Begin with a strong topic sentence that states your opinion.

3. Use the Writers' Checklist to revise.

Title:

V. WRAP-UP

What impressions, if any, did the selection make on you?

READERS'
CHECKLIST

MEANING
☐ Did you learn something from the reading?
☐ Did it affect you or make an impression?

Have you heard the phrase, "Give something the once over"? It means "Give it a quick look." It's a useful strategy to use when you are looking for an answer to a question. Giving a text a quick look is called skimming. You skim before you read to get a good idea of the subject of the selection.

Rosa Parks

BEFORE YOU READ

First look at the title, "Rosa Parks." It is the name of a real person. What do you already know about her?

1. List anything you already know about her below:

ROSA PARKS

2. Read each phrase below about Rosa Parks. Then skim through the selection. Look for information you need to complete the sentences. Try not to read each word or stop to reread.

Facts About Rosa Parks

Rosa Parks lived . . .

When Rosa Parks shopped, she . . .

Rosa Parks's job was . . .

When Rosa Parks got on the bus, she . . .

COLORED
WAITING ROOM
PRIVATE PROPERTY
NO PARKING
Driving Through or Turning Around

II. READ

Work with a partner. Before reading the selection, discuss the notes you made on the previous page.

1. Now read on. Take turns reading to each other.

2. Write in the Response Notes any **questions** you have.

R e s p o n s e   N o t e s

"Rosa Parks" (an interview) by Brian Lanker

As far back as I can remember, being black in Montgomery we were well aware of the <u>inequality</u> of our way of life. I hated it all the time. I didn't feel that in order to have some freedom, I should have to leave one part of the United States to go to another part of the same country just because one was South and one was North.

My mother believed in freedom and equality even though we didn't know it for reality during our life in Alabama.

EXAMPLE:
What does it mean that she "believed in freedom and equality"? How could she?

In some stores, if a woman wanted to go in to try a hat, they wouldn't be permitted to try it on unless they knew they were going to buy it, or they put a bag on the inside of it. In the shoe stores they had this long row of seats, and all of those in the front could be <u>vacant</u>, but if one of us would go in to buy, they'd always take you to the last one, to the back of the store. There were no black salespersons.

At the Montgomery Fair [a department store] I did men's <u>alterations</u>. Beginning in December coming up to the Christmas holiday, the work was a bit heavy. When I left the store that evening, I was tired, but I was tired every day. I had planned to get an electric heating pad so I could put some heat to my shoulder and my back and neck. After I stepped up on the bus, I noticed this driver as the same one who had evicted me from another bus way back in 1943.

VOCABULARY
inequality—condition in which some people are favored over others.
vacant—empty.
alterations—adjustments in clothing.

Just back of the whites there was a black man next to one vacant seat. So I sat down with him. A few white people boarded the bus and they found seats except this one man. That is when the bus driver looked at us and asked us to let him have those seats. After he saw we weren't moving immediately, he said "Y'all make it light on yourselves and let me have those seats."

Discuss the question with your partner. Then write your answer.

What's the bus driver saying to Rosa Parks?

....

....

....

When he saw that I was still remaining in the seat, the driver said, "If you don't stand up, I'm going to call the police and have you arrested." I said, "You may do that."

Two policemen came and wanted to know what was the trouble. One said, "Why don't you stand up?" I said, "I don't think I should have to." At that point I asked the policemen, "Why do you push us around?" He said, "I don't know, but the law is the law and you're under arrest."

The decision was made by the three of us, my husband, my mother, and me, that I would go on and use my case as a test case challenging segregation on the buses.

When I woke up the next morning and realized I had to go to work and it was pouring down rain, the first thing I thought about was the fact that I never would ride a segregated bus again. That was my decision for me and not necessarily for anybody else.

VOCABULARY

segregation—separation from others or from a main body or group.

Stop+Predict

What else will happen as a result of Rosa Parks's decision?

....

....

"Rosa Parks" continued

People just stayed off the buses because I was arrested, not because I asked them. If everybody else had been happy and doing well, my arrest wouldn't have made any difference at all.

The one thing I appreciated was the fact that when so many others, by the hundreds and by the thousands, joined in, there was a kind of lifting of a burden from me individually. I could feel that whatever my individual desires were to be free, I was not alone. There were many others who felt the same way.

The first thing that happened after the people stayed off was the black cab companies were willing to just charge bus fare instead of charging cab fare. Others who had any kind of car at all would give people rides. They had quite a transportation system set up. Mass meetings were keeping the <u>morale</u> up. They were singing and praying and raising money in the collection to buy gasoline or tires.

There was a lot of humor in it, too. Somebody told a story about a [white] husband who had fired the family cook because she refused to ride the bus to work. When his wife came home, she said, "If you don't go get her, you better be on your way." Some white people who were not wanting to be <u>deprived</u> of their <u>domestic</u> help would just go themselves and pick up the people who were working for them.

The officials really became furious when they saw that the rain and bad weather or distance or any other problem didn't matter.

VOCABULARY
morale—state of mind.
deprived—prevented from having.
domestic—relating to a home or household.

Many whites, even white Southerners, told me that even though it may have seemed like the blacks were being freed, they felt more free and at ease themselves. They thought that my action didn't just free blacks but them also.

Stop+Question

Why might Rosa Parks's action have made white people feel "more free"?

Some have suffered much more than I did. Some have even lost their lives. I just escaped some of the physical—maybe not all—but some of the physical pain. And the pain still remains. From back as far as I can remember.

When people made up their minds that they wanted to be free and took action, then there was a change. But they couldn't rest on just that change. It has to continue.

It just doesn't seem that an older person like I am should still have to be in the struggle, but if I have to be in it then I have no choice but to keep on.

I've been dreaming, looking, for as far back as I had any thought, of what it should be like to be a human being. My desires were to be free as soon as I had learned that there had been slavery of human beings and that I was a <u>descendant</u> from them. If there was a <u>proclamation</u> setting those who were slaves free, I thought they should be indeed free and not have any type of slavery put upon us.

VOCABULARY

descendant—person who comes from a particular ancestor or ancestors.
proclamation—public announcement; declaration.

Stop+Summarize

How would you describe what Rosa Parks did?

_____

_____

_____

GATHER YOUR THOUGHTS

A. ORGANIZE INFORMATION Use the organizer below to arrange information about Rosa Parks.

What Rosa did

How others feel about her

What she thinks

Rosa Parks

How I feel about her

B. OUTLINE YOUR SUBJECT Outlining helps writers plan what to say and helps readers follow the main ideas. The story about Rosa Parks can be outlined in this way.

Rosa Parks

I. Refused to give up her seat on the bus
   A. Riding home from work
   B. Tired from work and tired of discrimination
   C. Claimed open seat reserved for whites
   D. Was arrested

II. Inspired a protest movement
   A. Blacks stayed off buses
   B. Rallied community around her cause
   C. Changed the way blacks felt about themselves
   D. Began to change feelings about segregation

III. Showed what one's person's courage can do
   A. Touched people through her single act
   B. Became a positive force for change
   C. Improved way of life for black people

193

C. PLAN AN ESSAY Now plan a 3-paragraph essay about an event—something important you or someone you know did. It may help to refer to the outline of the Parks piece.

1. Complete the planner below for your essay. Answer each question.

2. Then add 2 details to support or explain your answer to each question.

Title:

I. What event will you write about?

Details:

    A.

    B.

II. What happened or changed because of it?

Details:

    A.

    B.

III. Why is what happened important to you?

Details:

    A.

    B.

IV. WRITE

Write a **3-paragraph essay** of your own about an event that was important to you.

1. Use your writing plan on the previous page.
2. Use the Writers' Checklist to revise.

Paragraph One—Introduction

Paragraph Two—Body

Continue your writing on the next page.

Paragraph Three—Conclusion

V. WRAP-UP

How, in your own words, would you explain why Rosa Parks's story is important?

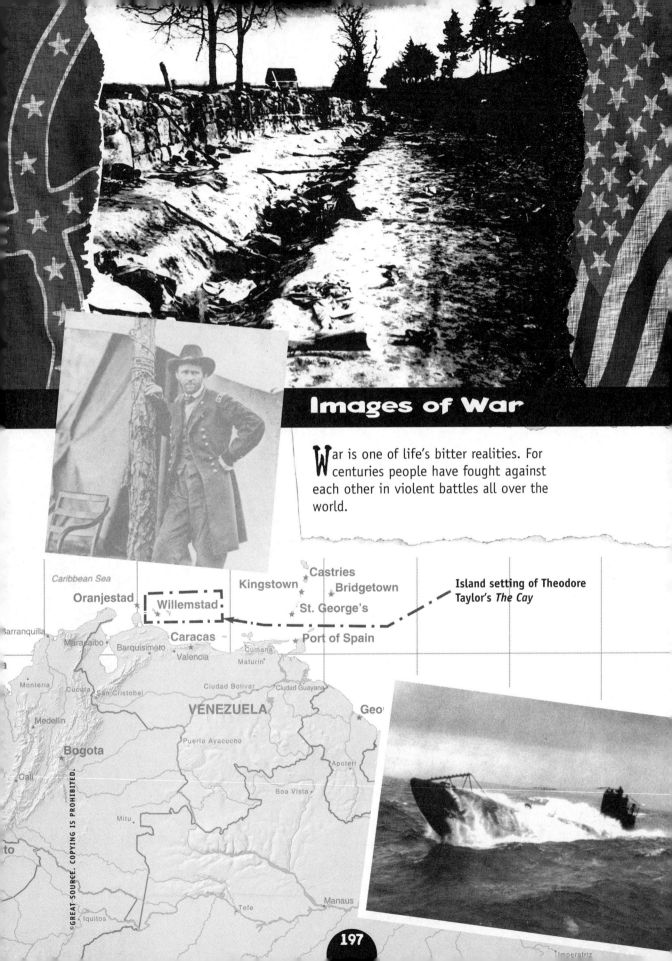

Images of War

War is one of life's bitter realities. For centuries people have fought against each other in violent battles all over the world.

Caribbean Sea

Oranjestad
Willemstad
Kingstown
Castries
Bridgetown
St. George's

Island setting of Theodore Taylor's *The Cay*

Barranquilla
Maracaibo
Barquisimeto
Caracas
Port of Spain
Valencia
Cumaná
Maturin

Monteria
Cúcuta
San Cristobal
Ciudad Bolívar
Ciudad Guayana

VENEZUELA
Geo

Medellin

Bogota
Puerto Ayacucho

Cali
Apoterí

Boa Vista

Mitú

Manaus

Tefe

Iquitos

21: A Taste of War

Three Confederate prisoners

Have you tried doing a picture walk before you read? It can help prepare you for what's to come. The drawings or photographs can give you that "yes, I know about this" feeling that is so important to understanding a story or article.

BEFORE YOU READ

Look at the photos on the pages in this lesson.
1. Read the captions and think about what the images suggest.
2. Make some predictions about the selection on the chart below.

PICTURE WALK

"A TASTE OF WAR"

I predict this story will be about:

who?

what?

where?

when?

why?

how?

I have these questions about the pictures:

1.

2.

3.

The photographs remind me of:

General Ulyssess S. Grant in 1864

READ

Now begin reading the following excerpt from the novel *The Red Badge of Courage*.

1. Pay special attention to what the characters say and do. Circle information about them that seems important.

2. Write your **reactions** to the characters in the Response Notes.

"A Taste of War" from *The Red Badge of Courage* by Stephen Crane

The (youth joined this crowd) and marched along with it. The torn bodies expressed the awful machinery in which the men had been entangled.

Orderlies and <u>couriers</u> occasionally broke through the <u>throng</u> in the roadway, scattering wounded men right and left, galloping on followed by <u>howls</u>. The <u>melancholy</u> march was continually disturbed by the messengers, and sometimes by bustling <u>batteries</u> that came swinging and thumping down upon them, the officers shouting orders to clear the way.

There was a <u>tattered</u> man, fouled with dust, blood and powder stain from hair to shoes, who trudged quietly at the youth's side. He was listening with eagerness and much humility to the <u>lurid</u> descriptions of a bearded sergeant. His lean features wore an expression of awe and admiration. He was like a listener in a country store to wondrous tales told among the sugar barrels. He eyed the story-teller with unspeakable wonder. His mouth was <u>agape in yokel fashion</u>.

RESPONSE NOTES

EXAMPLE:
Seems mysterious, like he doesn't fit in.

Major General William Tecumseh Sherman

VOCABULARY
couriers—messengers.
throng—large crowd.
howls—loud cries or screams.
melancholy—sad.
batteries—artillery units.
tattered—ragged.
lurid—shocking; horrific.
agape in yokel fashion—wide open; expressing the amazement of seeing something for the first time.

RESPONSE NOTES

The sergeant, taking note of this, gave pause to his elaborate history while he administered a <u>sardonic</u> comment. "Be keerful, honey, you'll be a-ketchin' flies," he said.

The tattered man shrank back <u>abashed</u>.

After a time he began to <u>sidle</u> near to the youth, and in a different way try to make him a friend. His voice was gentle as a girl's voice and his eyes were pleading. The youth saw with surprise that the soldier had two wounds, one in the head, bound with a blood-soaked rag, and the other in the arm, making that member dangle like a broken bough.

After they had walked together for some time the tattered man mustered sufficient courage to speak. "Was pretty good fight, wa'n't it?" he timidly said. The youth, deep in thought, glanced up at the bloody and grim figure with its lamblike eyes. "What?"

"Was pretty good fight, wa'n't it?"

Timeline

EARLIER

What occurred in the hours before this group of soldiers started walking?

....

....

....

....

....

....

....

....

NOW

How would you describe the soldiers now?

....

....

....

....

....

....

....

....

....

VOCABULARY
sardonic—scornful; mocking.
abashed—ashamed; uneasy.
sidle—move slowly.

"Yes," said the youth shortly. He quickened his pace.

But the other hobbled <u>industriously</u> after him. There was an air of apology in his manner, but he evidently thought that he needed only to talk for a time, and the youth would perceive that he was a good fellow.

"Was pretty good fight, wa'n't it?" he began in a small voice, and then he achieved the <u>fortitude</u> to continue. "Dern me if I ever see fellers fight so. Laws, how they did fight! I knowed th' boys'd like when they onct got square at it. Th' boys ain't had no fair chanct up t' now, but this time they showed what they was. I knowed it'd turn out this way. Yeh can't lick them boys. No, sir! They're fighters, they be."

Timeline

EARLIER

What is implied by the comment, "Th' boys ain't had no fair chanct up t' now . . ."?

FUTURE

What does the wounded man think will happen in the future?

VOCABULARY
industriously—diligently.
fortitude—strength of mind.

He breathed a deep breath of humble admiration. He had looked at the youth for encouragement several times. He received none, but gradually he seemed to get <u>absorbed</u> in his subject.

"I was <u>talkin' 'cross pickets</u> with a boy from Georgie, onct, an' that boy, he ses, 'Your fellers'll all run like hell when they onct hearn a gun,' he ses. <u>Mebbe</u> they will,' I ses, 'but I don't b'lieve none of it,' I ses; 'an' b'jiminey,' I ses back t' 'um, 'mebbe your fellers'll all run like hell when they onct hearn a gun,' I ses. He larfed. Well, they didn't run t'day, did they, hey? No, sir! They fit, an' fit, an' fit."

His homely face was <u>suffused</u> with a light of love for the army which was to him all things beautiful and powerful.

Timeline

FIRST

What did the boy from Georgia predict would happen when the fighting started?

....
....
....
....
....
....
....
....
....

NOW

What did happen, according to the wounded man, when the fighting started?

....
....
....
....
....
....
....
....
....

VOCABULARY
absorbed—deep into; fully engaged or interested in.
talkin' 'cross pickets—talking over a picket fence, as one might with a neighbor.
Mebbe—maybe.
suffused—filled.

"A Taste of War" CONTINUED

After a time he turned to the youth. "Where yeh hit, ol' boy?" he asked in a brotherly tone.

The youth felt instant <u>panic</u> at this question, although at first its full import was not borne in upon him.

"What?" he asked.

"Where yeh hit?" repeated the tattered man.

"Why," began the youth, "I—I—that is—why—I—"

He turned away suddenly and slid through the crowd. His brow was heavily flushed, and his fingers were picking nervously at one of his buttons. He bent his head and fastened his eyes <u>studiously</u> upon the button as if it were a little problem.

The tattered man looked after him in <u>astonishment</u>.

Timeline

FIRST

What question did the wounded man ask the youth?

NEXT

How did the youth feel when asked, "Where yeh hit"?

Why?

LAST

How did the youth respond?

VOCABULARY
panic—deep and sudden fear.
studiously—deeply and intently, as if studying a subject.
astonishment—complete surprise and wonder.

A. BRAINSTORM In this part of Crane's novel, the characters are never named. Yet it is easy to get a feel for who they are and what they are like. Use the character cluster below to make notes about the wounded man and the youth.

Confederate soldier

what he did

what he said

THE YOUTH

what he was like

what I thought about him

what he did

what he said

THE WOUNDED MAN

what he was like

what I thought about him

A group of Union soldiers camped out

B. DESCRIBE A CHARACTER Use the clusters from the previous page and skim through the selection again. Write a few words describing the youth and a few describing the wounded man.

youth

wounded man

C. PLAN Write a new opener for "A Taste of War" that will grab a reader's attention. Use the same characters and the same setting, but expand upon them. Add details. Start planning by answering the questions below.

HOW DOES THE YOUTH FEEL ABOUT THIS GROUP OF SOLDIERS?

HOW WERE THESE MEN WOUNDED?

WHERE ARE THEY GOING?

WHAT DO THEY EXPECT TO FIND ONCE THEY GET THERE?

IV. WRITE

Now write a new **story beginning** for "A Taste of War."

1. Try to use sensory details and dialogue to grab a reader's interest.

2. Use the Writers' Checklist to help you revise.

 V. ## WRAP-UP
What did "A Taste of War" make you think about?

READERS' CHECKLIST
DEPTH
☐ Did the reading make you think about things?
☐ Did it set off thoughts beyond the surface topic?

Walking through the text before you begin reading can familiarize you with what is to come. On a walk-through, look for special type (headlines, footnotes, blocks of dialogue) and pay special attention to titles and opening and closing paragraphs. Also keep an eye out for character and place names.

BEFORE YOU READ

Walk through the following excerpt from the novel *The Cay*. (A cay is an island.)

1. Make notes about the story on the chart below.

2. Refer to your chart when you begin your reading.

MY WALK-THROUGH OF "WAR COMES TO OUR ISLAND"

WHAT I LEARNED FROM READING THE FIRST PARAGRAPH:

CHARACTER NAMES:

PLACE NAMES:

THE SORT OF WORDS DEFINED IN THE FOOTNOTES:

WHAT I LEARNED FROM READING THE FINAL PARAGRAPH:

WHAT I THINK THE SELECTION WILL BE ABOUT:

READ

As you read this selection from the novel, keep an eye on the plot.
1. Write the main developments in the Story Frames.
2. In the Response Notes, list and **clarify** the main events.

"War Comes to Our Island" from *The Cay*
by Theodore Taylor

RESPONSE NOTES

Like silent, hungry sharks that swim in the darkness of the sea, the German submarines arrived in the middle of the night.

I was asleep on the second floor of our narrow, gabled green house in Willemstad, on the island of Curaçao, the largest of the Dutch islands just off the coast of Venezuela. I remember that on that moonless night in February 1942, they attacked the big Lago oil refinery on Aruba, the sister island west of us. Then they blew up six of our small lake tankers, the tubby ones that still bring crude oil from Lake Maracaibo to the refinery, Curaçaosche Petroleum Maatschappij, to be made into gasoline, kerosene, and diesel oil. One German sub was even sighted off Willemstad at dawn.

EXAMPLE:
1. German sub seen

Story Frame #1

Who or what arrives first? What happens next?

VOCABULARY
gabled—sloped-roof style.
Venezuela—country in South America.
crude oil—unrefined petroleum.
refinery—industrial plant for purifying crude oil.
kerosene—thin oil used as fuel.
diesel oil—special oil to fuel diesel engines.

A submarine surfacing

So when I woke up there was much excitement in the city, which looks like a part of old Holland, except that all the houses are painted in soft colors, pinks and greens and blues, and there are no dikes. It was very hard to finish my breakfast because I wanted to go to Punda, the business district, the oldest part of town, and then to Fort Amsterdam where I could look out to sea. If there was an enemy <u>U-boat</u> out there, I wanted to see it and join the people in shaking a fist at it.

I was not frightened, just terribly excited. War was something I'd heard a lot about, but had never seen. The whole world was at war, and now it had come to us in the warm, blue <u>Caribbean</u>.

The first thing that my mother said was, "Phillip, the enemy has finally attacked the island, and there will be no school today. But you must stay near home. Do you understand?"

I nodded, but I couldn't imagine that a shell from an enemy submarine would pick me out from all the buildings, or hit me if I was standing on the famous <u>pontoon bridge</u> or among the ships way back in the Schottegat or along St. Anna Bay.

Story Frame #2

Why didn't Phillip have school that day?

....

....

....

VOCABULARY
U-boat—submarine of the German navy.
Caribbean—sea by the coasts of Central and South America and the West Indies.
pontoon bridge—floating bridge.

"War Comes to Our Island" CONTINUED

RESPONSE NOTES

So later in the morning, when she was busy making sure that all our blackout curtains were in place, and filling extra pots with fresh water, and checking our food supply, I stole away down to the old fort with Henrik van Boven, my Dutch friend who was also eleven.

I had played there many times with Henrik and other boys when we were a few years younger, imagining we were defending Willemstad against pirates or even the British. They once stormed the island, I knew, long ago. Or sometimes we'd pretend we were the Dutch going out on raids against Spanish <u>galleons</u>. That had happened too. It was all so real that sometimes we could see the tall masted ships coming over the <u>horizon</u>.

Of course, they were only the tattered-sailed native <u>schooners</u> from Venezuela, Aruba, or Bonaire coming in with bananas, oranges, <u>papayas</u>, melons, and vegetables. But to us, they were always pirates, and we'd shout to the noisy black men aboard them. They'd laugh back and go, "Pow, pow, pow!"

Story Frame #3

Where did Phillip and his friend go?

....

....

....

....

The fort looks as though it came out of a storybook, with gun ports along the high wall that faces the sea. For years, it guarded Willemstad. But this one morning, it did not look like a storybook fort at all. There were

Submarine periscope

VOCABULARY
galleons—large sailing ships used long ago.
horizon—place in the distance where the earth and sky appear to meet.
schooners—sailing vessels with at least two masts.
papayas—kind of yellow fruit.

real soldiers with rifles and we saw machine guns. Men with <u>binoculars</u> had them trained toward the whitecaps, and everyone was tense. They chased us away, telling us to go home.

Instead, we went down to the Koningin Emma Brug, the famous Queen Emma pontoon bridge, which spans the channel that leads to the huge harbor, the Schottegat. The bridge is built on floats so that it can swing open as ships pass in or out, and it connects Punda with Otrabanda, which means "other side," the other part of the city.

Story Frame #4

What did Phillip and Henrik find at the fort? Why didn't they stay there?

....

....

....

....

The view from there wasn't as good as from the fort, but curious people were there, too, just looking. Strangely, no ships were moving in the channel. The *veerboots*, the ferry boats that shuttled cars and people back and forth when the bridge was swung open, were tied up and empty. Even the native schooners were quiet against the docks inside the channel. And the black men were not laughing and shouting the way they usually did.

Henrik said, "My father told me there is nothing left of Aruba. They hit Sint Nicolaas, you know."

"Every lake tanker was sunk," I said.

VOCABULARY
binoculars—device for making distant objects appear closer.

"War Comes to Our Island" CONTINUED

I didn't know if that were true or not, but Henrik had an irritating way of sounding official since his father was connected with the government.

His face was round and he was chubby. His hair was straw-colored and his cheeks were always red. Henrik was very serious about everything he said or did. He looked toward Fort Amsterdam.

He said, "I bet they put big guns up there now."

That was a safe bet.

And I said, "It won't be long until the Navy is here."

Henrik looked at me. "Our Navy?" He meant the Netherlands Navy.

"No," I said. "Ours." Meaning the American Navy, of course. His little Navy was scattered all over after the Germans took Holland.

Henrik said quietly, "Our Navy will come too," and I didn't want to argue with him. Everyone felt bad that Holland had been conquered by the Nazis.

American submarine

Then an army officer climbed out of a truck and told us all to leave the Queen Emma bridge. He was very stern. He growled, "Don't you know they could shoot a <u>torpedo</u> up here and kill you all?"

I looked out toward the sea again. It was blue and peaceful, and a good breeze churned it up, making lines of whitecaps. White clouds drifted slowly over it. But I couldn't see the usual parade of ships coming toward the harbor; the stubby ones or the massive ones with

VOCABULARY

torpedo—weapon that moves under water, fired from a submarine.

RESPONSE NOTES

flags of many nations that steamed slowly up the bay to the Schottegat to load gas and oil.

The sea was empty; there was not even a sail on it. We suddenly became frightened and ran home to the Scharloo section where we lived.

I guess my face was pale when I went into the house because my mother, who was in the kitchen, asked immediately, "Where have you been?"

"Punda," I admitted. "I went with Henrik."

My mother got very upset. She grabbed my shoulder and shook it. "I told you not to go there, Phillip," she said angrily. "We are at war! Don't you understand?"

Story Frame #5

What causes the boys to become frightened?

....

....

....

Submarine surfacing

GATHER YOUR THOUGHTS

A. EVALUATE Get ready to write a review of "War Comes to Our Island." In a review, you state your opinion and then support it with facts and details from what you're reviewing. Most literary reviews focus on 1 or more of the 4 main elements of fiction:
• the plot
• the characters
• the setting
• the theme
Use the scales below to rate "War Comes to Our Island."

DIRECTIONS: SCORE "WAR COMES TO OUR ISLAND" ON EACH OF THESE SCALES. CIRCLE THE RATING THAT REFLECTS YOUR OPINION.

The plot is . . .

1   2   3   4   5   6   7   8   9   10

very   sort of   not at all
interesting   interesting   interesting

The characters are . . .

1   2   3   4   5   6   7   8   9   10

easy to   somewhat   not easy to
relate to   easy to   relate to
              relate to

The setting is . . .

1   2   3   4   5   6   7   8   9   10

well   fairly well   not at all
developed   developed   well
                                     developed

The theme is . . .

1   2   3   4   5   6   7   8   9   10

well   fairly well   not at all
developed   developed   well
                                     developed

B. REFLECT Reflect on what you read. Think about what you want to say about different parts of what you read.

What I liked best is

_____

_____

What I liked least is

_____

_____

C. ORGANIZE YOUR THOUGHTS Begin to plan a 1-paragraph review of "War Comes to Our Island." Focus your review on 1 aspect of Taylor's story: the plot, characters, setting, or theme.

1. Write a topic sentence that states your opinion.

(circle one)

Focus: plot   characters   setting   theme

Topic sentence:

_____

_____

2. Then write 2–3 details to support your topic sentence.

My details:

1. _____

2. _____

3. _____

WRITE

IV.

Now you are ready to write your **review**.
1. Begin with the topic sentence, which should make clear your overall opinion.
2. Then add details to support your opinion.
3. Use the Writers' Checklist to help you revise.

WRITERS' CHECKLIST
TITLES

❑ **Did you use quotation marks around the titles of chapters or subdivisions of books, poems, short stories, and newspaper and magazine articles?** EXAMPLES: *"It's Quiet Now"* *is a powerful short story. I just read Carolina Hospital's poem "Papa."*

❑ **Did you underline or use italics for titles of books, films, long poems, magazines, and newspapers?** EXAMPLES: *The Great Gatsby is a marvelous book. We need to read Time and Newsweek for our history project. The Cay was written by Theodore Taylor.*

What did you notice about Theodore Taylor's writing style?

Isaac Asimov

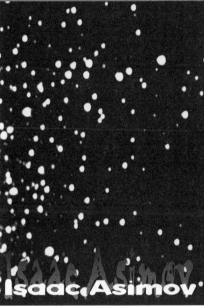

Isaac Asimov

Isaac Asimov (1920–1992) was born in Russia and moved to the United States at age three. He studied and taught biochemistry before becoming a full-time writer in 1958. Asimov's interest in science carried over into much of his writing—nonfiction, novels, essays, and short stories. Asimov is recognized as one of the greatest science fiction writers ever.

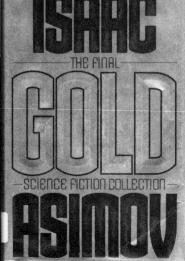

ISAAC
THE FINAL
GOLD
SCIENCE FICTION COLLECTION
ASIMOV

What are the causes of war? In his story "Frustration," Isaac Asimov explores the idea of self-righteousness and war. Self-righteousness is having the sense of being morally superior to others.

BEFORE YOU READ

A character from the following story implies that wars are caused by self-righteousness. Do you agree? First, you will need to understand the word *self-righteousness*. Read the definition below and then brainstorm other words, ideas, or situations related to it.

self-righteousness

—filled with a sense or showing that one thinks oneself to be morally superior to others

READ

Read "Frustration" with a partner. Take turns reading aloud.

1. As you read, if you don't understand part of the story, jot a **question** in the Response Notes.

2. Pay special attention to characters who think they are superior to others.

"Frustration" by Isaac Asimov

Herman Gelb turned his head to watch the departing figure. Then he said, "Wasn't that the Secretary?"

"Yes, that was the Secretary of Foreign Affairs. Old man Hargrove. Are you ready for lunch?"

"Of course. What was he doing here?"

Peter Jonsbeck didn't answer immediately. He merely stood up, and beckoned Gelb to follow. They walked down the corridor and into a room that had the steamy smell of spicy food.

"Here you are," said Jonsbeck. "The whole meal has been prepared by computer. Completely automated. Untouched by human hands. And my own programming. I promised you a treat, and here you are."

It *was* good. Gelb could not deny it and didn't want to. Over dessert, he said, "But what was Hargrove doing here?"

Jonsbeck smiled. "Consulting me on programming. What else am I good for?"

"But why? Or is it something you can't talk about?"

RESPONSE NOTES

EXAMPLE:
Where are they?
And when—what
year?

VOCABULARY

beckoned—invited; called.
corridor—narrow hallway.
spicy—flavorful.
automated—operated by machine.
programming—system of codes for a computer.

What is Jonsbeck's job?

What can you tell about the society described in this story?

"Frustration" continued

"It's something I suppose I *shouldn't* talk about, but it's a fairly open secret. There isn't a computer man in the capital who doesn't know what the poor frustrated simp is up to."

"What is he up to then?"

"He's fighting wars."

Gelb's eyes opened wide. "With whom?"

"With nobody, really. He fights them by computer analysis. He's been doing it for I don't know how long."

"But why?"

"He wants the world to be the way we are—noble, honest, decent, full of respect for human rights and so on."

"So do I. So do we all. We have to keep up the pressure on the bad guys, that's all."

"And they're keeping the pressure on us, too. They don't think we're perfect."

"I suppose we're not, but we're better than they are. You know that."

Jonsbeck shrugged. "A difference in point of view. It doesn't matter. We've got a world to run, space to develop, computerization to extend. Cooperation puts a premium on continued cooperation and there is slow improvement. We'll get along. It's just that Hargrove

VOCABULARY
simp—simple or foolish person.
analysis—close study of something.
premium—unusually high value.

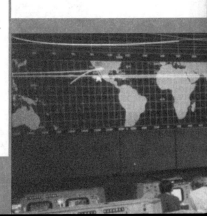

"Frustration" continued

doesn't want to wait. He <u>hankers</u> for quick improvement—by force. You know, *make* the bums shape up. We're strong enough to do it."

"By force? By war, you mean. We don't fight wars any more."

"That's because it's gotten too <u>complicated</u>. Too much danger. We're all too powerful. You know what I mean? Except that Hargrove thinks he can find a way. You punch certain starting conditions into the computer and let it fight the war mathematically and yield the results."

STOP AND PREDICT

Why does Hargrove favor war? Will he succeed?

STOP AND PREDICT

"How do you make equations for war?"

"Well, you try, old man. Men. Weapons. Surprise. <u>Counterattack</u>. Ships. Space stations. Computers. We mustn't forget computers. There are a hundred factors and thousands of <u>intensities</u> and millions of combinations. Hargrove thinks it is possible to find *some* combination of starting conditions and courses of development that will result in clear victory for us and not too much damage to the world, and he labors under constant frustration."

"But what if he gets what he wants?"

"Well, if he can find the combination—if the computer says, 'This is it,' then I suppose he thinks he can argue our government into fighting exactly the war the computer has worked out so that, <u>barring random</u>

VOCABULARY

hankers—strongly desires.
complicated—not easy to understand, deal with, or solve.
Counterattack—return attack.
intensities—degrees of strength.
barring random—assuming no unexpected.

events that upset the indicated course, we'd have what we want."

"There'd be <u>casualties</u>."

"Yes, of course. But the computer will presumably compare the casualties and other damage—to the economy and ecology, for instance—to the benefits that would derive from our control of the world, and if it decides the benefits will outweigh the casualties, then it will give the go-ahead for a 'just war.' After all, it may be that even the losing nations would benefit from being directed by us, with our stronger economy and stronger moral sense."

Gelb stared his disbelief and said, "I never knew we were sitting at the lip of a <u>volcanic crater</u> like that. What about the 'random events' you mentioned?"

"The computer program tries to allow for the unexpected, but you never can, of course. So I don't think the go-ahead will come. It hasn't so far, and unless old man Hargrove can present the government with a computer <u>simulation</u> of a war that is totally satisfactory, I don't think there's much chance he can force one."

"And he comes to you, then, for what reason?"

"To improve the program, of course."

"And you help him?"

"Yes, certainly. There are big fees involved, Herman."

VOCABULARY
casualties—people killed or injured during a military operation.
volcanic crater—hollow area shaped like a bowl at the mouth of a volcano.
simulation—representation of an actual operation.

"Frustration" continued

Gelb shook his head, "Peter! Are you going to try to arrange a war, just for money?"

"There won't be a war. There's no realistic combination of events that would make the computer decide on war. Computers place a greater value on human lives than human beings do themselves, and what will seem <u>bearable</u> to Secretary Hargrove, or even to you and me, will never be passed by a computer."

STOP AND REFLECT

Jonsbeck says, "Computers place a greater value on human lives than human beings do themselves. . . ." What does this mean?

....

....

....

STOP AND REFLECT

"How can you be sure of that?"

"Because I'm a programmer and I don't know of any way of programming a computer to give it what is most needed to start any war, any persecution, any devilry, while ignoring any harm that may be done in the process. And because it lacks what is most needed, the computers will always give Hargrove, and all others who hanker for war, nothing but frustration."

"What is it that a computer doesn't have, then?"

"Why, Gelb. It totally lacks a sense of self-righteousness."

VOCABULARY
bearable—manageable.

STOP AND SUMMARIZE STOP AND SUMMARIZE

What is "Frustration" about?

....

....

....

....

III GATHER YOUR THOUGHTS

A. SUMMARIZE Use the organizer below to summarize what you read in "Frustration."

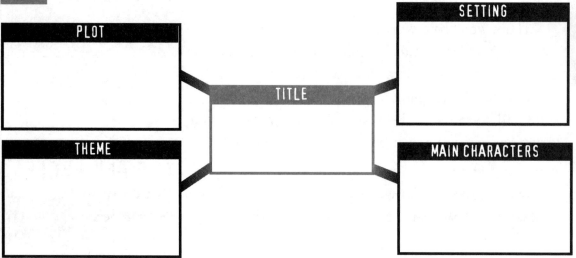

PLOT

SETTING

TITLE

THEME

MAIN CHARACTERS

B. QUICKWRITE Do you agree with Isaac Asimov that wars are caused by self-righteousness? Think about this question and then jot down your ideas as you quickwrite.

1. Spend 1-3 minutes writing down whatever comes to mind.

2. Write without stopping. Your goal should be to explore your thoughts, not to worry about spelling and punctuation.

CAUSES OF WAR

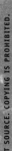

IV. WRITE

Now write a **journal entry** that explores other ideas about the causes of war.

1. In your entry, reflect on what causes wars. Use specific details, such as examples from history or current events, to explain your opinion.

2. Use the Writers' Checklist to help you revise.

WRITERS' CHECKLIST

COMMAS

❏ Did you use commas to separate items in a series? EXAMPLE: *I am hot, tired, and hungry.* (Do not put a comma after the and before the last item.)

❏ Did you use commas to set off a quotation from the rest of the sentence? EXAMPLE: *"Don't program the computer," the man yelled.*

V. WRAP-UP

What made the story easy or hard to read?

READERS' CHECKLIST

EASE

❏ Was the passage easy to read?

❏ Were you able to read it smoothly and without difficulty?

WORD WEB

What do you want to be? What sort of work do you want to do? Ever wonder whose job it is to write all of those science fiction stories about far-off galaxies?

I. **BEFORE YOU READ**

In "Hints," Isaac Asimov gives tips for writing stories.
1. Think about how you feel when you have to write a story. What tips would you give someone?
2. Record your ideas about writing a story on the web below.

How to write a story

READ

Read the article at your own pace.
1. Circle anything you find surprising or have a strong reaction to.
2. As you read, **mark** or **highlight** in the Response Notes the 3-4 things you need to be a successful writer.

"Hints" by Isaac Asimov

Every once in a short while I get a letter from some eager young would-be writer asking me for some "hints" on the art of writing science fiction.

The feeling I have is that my correspondents think there is some magic formula jealously guarded by the professionals, but that since I'm such a nice guy I will spill the beans if properly approached.

Alas, there's no such thing, no magic formula, no secret tricks, no hidden short-cuts.

I'm sorry to have to tell you that it's a matter of hard work over a long period of time. If you know of any exceptions to this, that's exactly what they are—exceptions.

RESPONSE NOTES

EXAMPLE:
1. Hard work

WORD · ATTACK

TIP 1: USE WORD PARTS. *Correspondents* has two parts. *Correspond* means "to communicate." The suffix *-ent* can mean "someone who."

Correspondents means
....
....

There are, however, some general principles that could be useful, to my way of thinking, and here they are:

1) You have to prepare for a career as a successful

VOCABULARY
jealously—enviously, with a fear that something may be taken away.
exceptions—things other than; exclusions.

RESPONSE NOTES

science fiction writer—as you would for any other highly specialized calling.

First, you have to learn to use your tools, just as a surgeon has to learn to use his.

The basic tool for any writer is the English language, which means you must develop a good vocabulary and brush up on such prosaic things as spelling and grammar.

There can be little argument about vocabulary, but it may occur to you that spelling and grammar are just frills. After all, if you write great and gorgeous stories, surely the editor will be delighted to correct your spelling and grammar.

Not so! He (or she) won't be.

WORD ATTACK

TIP 2: USE CONTEXT CLUES. What does the word prosaic mean?

....

....

....

Besides, take it from an old war-horse, if your spelling and grammar are rotten, you won't be writing a great and gorgeous story. Someone who can't use a saw and hammer doesn't turn out stately furniture.

Even if you've been diligent at school, have developed a vocabulary, can spell "sacrilege" and "supersede" and never say "between you and I" or "I

VOCABULARY
specialized—trained in one specific area.
surgeon—doctor who operates on people.
gorgeous—extremely beautiful.
old war-horse—someone with much experience.
diligent—hard-working; tireless.
sacrilege—destruction or misuse of something holy or sacred.
supersede—take the place of.

"Hints" continued

ain't never done nothing," that's still not enough. There's the subtle structure of the English sentence and the artful construction of the English paragraph. There is the clever <u>interweaving</u> of plot, the handling of <u>dialogue</u>, and a thousand other intricacies.

How do you learn that? Do you read books on how to write, or attend classes on writing, or go to writing conferences? These are all of <u>inspirational</u> value, I'm sure, but they won't teach you what you really want to know.

What *will* teach you is the careful reading of the masters of English prose. This does not mean condemning yourself to years of falling asleep over dull <u>classics</u>. Good writers are invariably fascinating writers—the two go together. In my opinion, the English writers who most clearly use the correct word every time and who most artfully and <u>deftly</u> put together their sentences and paragraphs are Charles Dickens, Mark Twain, and P. G. Wodehouse.

Read them, and others, but with attention. They represent your schoolroom. Observe what they do and try to figure out why they do it. It's no use other people explaining it to you; until you see it for yourself and it becomes part of you, nothing will help.

But suppose that no matter how you try, you can't seem to absorb the lesson. Well, it may be that you're not a writer. It's no disgrace. You can always go on to take up some slightly <u>inferior</u> profession like surgery or the presidency of the United States. It won't be as good, of course; but we can't all scale the heights.

VOCABULARY
interweaving—blending together; mixing.
dialogue—conversation between two or more people.
inspirational—exciting to the mind or emotions.
classics—literary works regarded as excellent models and standards of study.
deftly—quickly and skillfully.
inferior—lower in quality; second-rate.

Second, for a science fiction writing career, it is not enough to know the English language; you also have to know science. You may not want to use much science in your stories; but you'll have to know it anyway, so that what you do use, you don't misuse.

This does not mean you have to be a professional scientist, or a science major at college. You don't even have to go to college. It does mean, though, that you have to be willing to study science on your own, if your formal education has been weak in that direction.

It's not impossible. One of the best writers of hard science fiction is Fred Pohl, and he never even finished high school. Of course, there are very few people who are as bright as Fred, but you can write considerably less well than he does and still be pretty good.

Fortunately, there is more good, popular-science writing these days than there was in previous generations, and you can learn a great deal, rather painlessly, if you read such science fiction writers as L. Sprague de Camp, Ben Bova, and Poul Anderson in their nonfictional moods—or even Isaac Asimov.

WORD ATTACK

What do you think the word <u>painlessly</u> means? Say it slowly to yourself.

....

....

What's more, professional scientists are also writing effectively for the public these days, as witness Carl Sagan's magnificent books. And there's always *Scientific American*.

Third, even if you know your science and your writing, it is still not likely that you will be able to put them together from scratch. You will have to be a

"Hints" continued

diligent reader of science fiction itself to learn the conventions and the tricks of the trade—how to interweave background and plot, for instance.

2) You have to work at the job.

The final bit of schooling is writing itself. Nor must you wait till your preparation is complete. The act of writing is itself part of the preparation.

You can't completely understand what good writers do until you try it yourself. You learn a great deal when you find your story breaking apart in your hands—or beginning to hang together. Write from the very beginning, then, and keep on writing.

3) You have to be patient.

Since writing is itself a schooling, you can't very well expect to sell the first story you write. (Yes, I know Bob Heinlein did it, but he was Bob Heinlein. You are only you.)

But then, why should that discourage you? After you finished the first grade at school, you weren't through, were you? You went on to the second grade, then the third, then the fourth, and so on.

If each story you write is one more step in your literary education, a rejection shouldn't matter. [Editors don't reject writers; they reject pieces of paper that have been typed on. Ed.] The next story will be better, and the next one after that still better, and eventually—

But then why bother to submit the stories? If you don't, how can you possibly know when you graduate? After all, you don't know which story you'll sell.

You might even sell the first. You almost certainly won't, but you just might.

Of course, even after you sell a story, you may fail to place the next dozen, but having done it once, it is quite likely that you will eventually do it again, if you persevere.

VOCABULARY
conventions—widely accepted practices or customs.

RESPONSE NOTES

But what if you write and write and write and you don't seem to be getting any better and all you collect are printed rejection slips? Once again, it may be that you are not a writer and will have to settle for a lesser post such as that of chief justice of the Supreme Court.

Look at the word <u>persevere</u> on the previous page. What do you think it means? Say it slowly to yourself.

....

....

....

4) You have to be reasonable.

Writing is the most wonderful and satisfying task in the world, but it does have one or two <u>insignificant flaws</u>. Among those flaws is the fact that a writer can almost never make a living at it.

Oh, a few writers make a lot of money—they're the ones we all hear about. But for every writer who rakes it in, there are a thousand who dread the monthly rent bill. It shouldn't be like that, but it is.

Take my case. Three years after I sold my first story, I reached the stage of selling everything I wrote, so that I had become a successful writer. Nevertheless, it took me seventeen more years as a *successful* writer before I could actually support myself in comfort on my earnings as a writer.

So while you're trying to be a writer, make sure you find another way of making a decent living—and don't quit your job after you make your first sale.

VOCABULARY
insignificant flaws—unimportant mistakes.

GATHER YOUR THOUGHTS

A. BRAINSTORM Science fiction stories are made up. But they are often based on a bit of science, such as computers, space travel, medicine, and so on.

1. Think of something scientific—a piece of equipment (like a microscope), a process (like freezing), or an invention (like the telephone). Use the science word you choose as the basis for a story.

2. Brainstorm words and ideas about your scientific word.

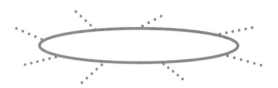

B. DEVELOP A CHARACTER Your story will feature a main character. Think of a name for a character that you will link to your scientific word. Then answer the questions below.

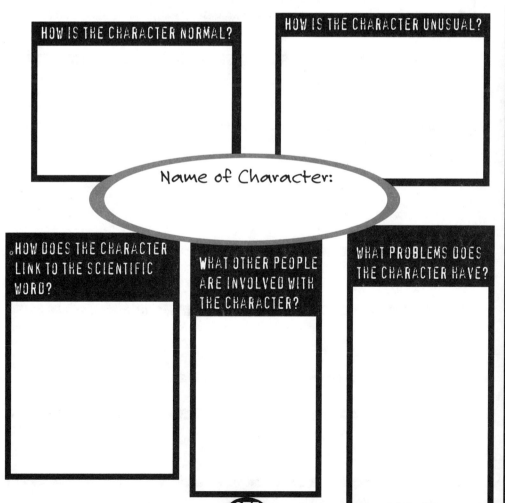

HOW IS THE CHARACTER NORMAL?

HOW IS THE CHARACTER UNUSUAL?

Name of Character:

HOW DOES THE CHARACTER LINK TO THE SCIENTIFIC WORD?

WHAT OTHER PEOPLE ARE INVOLVED WITH THE CHARACTER?

WHAT PROBLEMS DOES THE CHARACTER HAVE?

C. PLOT THE STORY. Now plan your story. Use the Plot Chart below to record the setting and characters. List the major events in the story. Write the events in chronological order, from beginning to end.

CHARACTERS

SETTING

WRITE

Write your own **science fiction story** to entertain your friends.

1. Use the notes you made about plot and character.

2. Give your story a title.

3. Use the Writers' Checklist to help you revise.

Continue your writing on the next page.

WRITERS' CHECK LIST

CAPITALIZATION

☐ Did you capitalize the names of specific buildings, monuments, institutions, companies, and groups? EXAMPLES: *White House, Statue of Liberty, University of Chicago, Microsoft, Boy Scouts of America*

☐ Did you capitalize the names of ethnic groups, national groups, and languages? EXAMPLES: *Latino, Vietnamese, British, Swahili*

☐ Did you capitalize the names of planets, continents, countries, states, counties, and cities? EXAMPLES: *Jupiter, South America, Nigeria, Michigan, Kendall County, Austin*

V. WRAP-UP

What did you most enjoy reading in Asimov's story?

Acknowledgments

13 "High School: The Bad and the Good" from AMERICAN ISLAM. Copyright ©1994 by Richard Wormser. Reprinted with permission from Walker and Company, 435 Hudson Street, New York, New York 10014. All Rights Reserved.

21 "Finding Patrick" by Paul Galloway/Copyrighted Chicago Tribune Company. All rights reserved, used with permission.

35 "It's Quiet Now" by Gcina Mhlope. Originally published in SOMETIMES WHEN IT RAINS: WRITINGS BY SOUTH AFRICAN WOMEN, edited by Ann Oosthuizen, Pandora Press.

42 "Survival" by Mark Mathabane. Reprinted with the permission of Simon and Schuster from KAFFIR BOY by Mark Mathabane. Copyright ©1986 by Mark Mathabane.

53 "How it Feels to Be Colored Me" by Zora Neale Hurston. Used with the permission of the Estate of Zora Neale Hurston.

65 "The Eatonville Anthology" by Zora Neale Hurston. Excerpts from "The Eatonville Anthology" as taken from THE COMPLETE STORIES by ZORA NEALE HURSTON. Introduction copyright ©1995 by Henry Louis Gates, Jr., and Sieglinde Lemke. Compilation copyright ©1995 by Vivian Bowden, Lois J. Hurston Gaston, Clifford Hurston, Lucy Ann Hurston, Winifred Hurston Clark, Zora Mack Goins, Edgar Hurston, Sr., and Barbara Hurston Lewis. Afterward and Bibliography copyright ©1995 by Henry Louis Gates. Reprinted by permission of HarperCollins Publishers, Inc.

74 "Visit to Africa" from ALL GOD'S CHILDREN NEED TRAVELING SHOES by Maya Angelou. Copyright ©1986 by Maya Angelou. Reprinted by permission of Random House, Inc.

83, 84 "Dear Tía" and "Papa" by Carolina Hospital. "Dear Tía" and "Papa" by Carolina Hospital are reprinted with permission from the publisher of *Decade II: A Twentieth Anniversary Anthology* (Houston: Arte Público Press University of Houston, 1993).

88 "The Guest Who Ran Away" from ARAB FOLK TALES by Inea Bushnaq. Copyright ©1986 by Inea Bushnaq. Reprinted by permission of Pantheon Books, a division of Random House, Inc.

95, 97 "The Price of Pride" and "How Si' Djeha Staved Off Hunger" from ARAB FOLK TALES by Inea Bushnaq. Copyright ©1986 by Inea Bushnaq. Reprinted by permission of Pantheon Books, a division of Random House, Inc.

107 "Puerto Rican Paradise" from DOWN THESE MEAN STREETS by Piri Thomas. Copyright ©1967 by Piri Thomas. Reprinted by permission of Alfred A. Knopf, Inc.

115 "If You Ain't Got Heart, You Ain't Got Nada" from DOWN THESE MEAN STREETS by Piri Thomas. Copyright ©1967 by Piri Thomas. Reprinted by permission of Alfred A. Knopf, Inc.

125 "Her Life Was Not a Joke" by Bob Greene. Copyright © 1997 by John Deadline Enterprises, Inc.

135 "One Morning," excerpt from Chapter 1 "Thornhill" from FREE THE CHILDREN by Craig Kielburger with Kevin Major. Copyright ©1998 by Craig Kielburger. Reprinted by permission of HarperCollins Publishers, Inc.

144 "The Knight in Person" from KNIGHTS by Julek Heller. Copyright ©1982 by Bellow & Highton Publishers Ltd.

153 "The Victorious Feudal Knight" by Jay Williams. Reprinted by permission of *Forbes Magazine.* ©1999 Forbes 1962.

163, 164 "Forgetfulness" and "An Unwritten Letter" from ECHOES OF AN AUTOBIOGRAPHY by Naguib Mahfouz. Translation copyright ©1997 by The American University of Cairo Press. Foreword ©1997 by Nadine Gordimer. Used by permission of Doubleday, a division of Random House, Inc.

171, 172 "A Man Reserves a Seat" and "Justice" from ECHOES OF AN AUTOBIOGRAPHY by Naguib Mahfouz. Translation copyright ©1997 by The American University of Cairo Press. Foreword ©1997 by Nadine Gordimer. Used by permission of Doubleday, a division of Random House, Inc.

189 "Rosa Parks" from I DREAM A WORLD: PORTRAITS OF BLACK WOMEN WHO CHANGED AMERICA by Brian Lanker. Copyright ©1989 by Brian Lanker.

209 "War Comes to Our Island" from THE CAY by Theodore Taylor. Copyright ©1969 by Theodore Taylor. Used by permission of Doubleday, a division of Random House, Inc.

221 "Frustration" by Isaac Asimov. © 1991 Nightfall, Inc. Published by permission of the Estate of Isaac Asimov, c/o Ralph M. Vicinanza.

229 "Hints" by Isaac Asimov. © 1979 Nightfall, Inc. Published by permission of the Estate of Isaac Asimov, c/o Ralph M. Vicinanza.

Photography:

COVER: All photos © Eileen Ryan.

TABLE OF CONTENTS and INTRODUCTION: All photos © Eileen Ryan except where noted. Page 3: lower right, background—courtesy Library of Congress. Page 4: background—courtesy Library of Congress, center—courtesy National Archive. Page 5: background, lower left, upper left, center—courtesy Library of Congress. Page 6: center—courtesy Library of Congress. Page 10: upper right—courtesy National Archive, lower left—courtesy Library of Congress.

CHAPTER 1: All photos ©Eileen Ryan except where noted. Page 11: lower left—courtesy Library of Congress. Page 20: upper right—Al Meyers. Pages 21–24: courtesy Library of Congress. Page 26: background—courtesy Library of Congress. Page 27: lower right—courtesy Library of Congress. Page 28: courtesy Library of Congress. Page 29: background, lower left—courtesy Library of Congress. Page 30: center—courtesy Library of Congress. Page 31: background—courtesy Library of Congress. Page 32:—courtesy Library of Congress.

CHAPTER 2: All photos courtesy Library of Congress except where noted. Page 33: Mandela photo—©AP/Wide World Photos, top—Al Meyers. Page 35: Al Meyers. Page 38: bottom—Al Meyers. Page 42: Al Meyers. Page 46: lower left—Al Meyers. Pages 48–49: ©Eileen Ryan. Page 50: bottom—Al Meyers.

CHAPTER 3: All photos courtesy Library of Congress except where noted. Page 58: ©Eileen Ryan. Page 61: ©Eileen Ryan. Page 62: background—©Eileen Ryan. Page 63: lower left—©Eileen Ryan. Page 67: ©Eileen Ryan

Acknowledgments continued

CHAPTER 4: All photos © Eileen Ryan except where noted. Page 74: top—courtesy Library of Congress. Page 76: lower left—courtesy Library of Congress. Page 77: lower right—courtesy Library of Congress. Page 80: upper right—courtesy Library of Congress.

CHAPTER 5: All photos courtesy Library of Congress except where noted. Page 88: top—courtesy National Archive. Page 94: courtesy National Archive. Page 95: lower right—courtesy National Archive. Page 99: courtesy National Archive. Page 100: top—courtesy National Archive. Page 109: background—courtesy National Archive.

CHAPTER 6: All photos © Eileen Ryan except where noted. Page 105: author photo—©Chris Lawrence/Courtesy of Piri Thomas lower right—courtesy Library of Congress, Page 109: lower right—courtesy Library of Congress. Page 111: center—courtesy Library of Congress. Page 112: background—courtesy Library of Congress. Page 114: lower right—courtesy Library of Congress. Page 115: upper left—courtesy Library of Congress. Page 121: upper left—courtesy Library of Congress.

CHAPTER 7: All photos courtesy Library of Congress except where noted. Page 123: upper right—©Eileen Ryan. Pages 124, 126, 130, 131, 132, 134, 135, 138: ©Eileen Ryan. Page 127: top—©Eileen Ryan. Page 133: background, lower right—©Eileen Ryan.

CHAPTER 8: All photos courtesy Library of Congress except where noted. Page 143: bottom—©Eileen Ryan, center—©Claudia Kunin/Tony Stone Images. Page 144: bottom—©Eileen Ryan. Page 157: bottom—©Eileen Ryan. Page 159: bottom—©Eileen Ryan. Page 160: lower left—©Eileen Ryan.

CHAPTER 9: All photos courtesy Library of Congress except where noted. Page 161: center, lower left,—©Eileen Ryan, book cover—From ECHOES OF AN AUTOBIOGRAPHY by Naguib Mahfouz. Copyright. Used by permission of Doubleday, a division of Random House, Inc. Page 164: upper right—©Eileen Ryan. Page 165: lower left—©Eileen Ryan. Page 166: bottom—©Eileen Ryan. Page

169: lower left—©Eileen Ryan, center—courtesy National Archive. Page 170: lower right—©Eileen Ryan. Page 173: upper right—©Eileen Ryan. Page 174: upper left—©Eileen Ryan.

CHAPTER 10: All photos courtesy Library of Congress except where noted. Page 180: ©Eileen Ryan.

CHAPTER 11: All photos courtesy Library of Congress except where noted. Page 208: background—©Eileen Ryan. Page 210: background—©Eileen Ryan. Page 214: lower right—©Eileen Ryan. Page 215: upper left—©Eileen Ryan. Page 216: upper right—©Eileen Ryan. Page 218: top—©Eileen Ryan.

CHAPTER 12: All photos © Eileen Ryan except where noted.

Page 219: NASA, except; center—©John Olson/Gamma-Liason. Page 220: top, background—courtesy Library of Congress, inset—NASA. Page 221: inset—NASA. Pages 222–225: NASA. Page 226: background—courtesy Library of Congress, inset NASA. Page 227: background—NASA, inset—courtesy Library of Congress.

Cover and Book Design:
Christine Ronan and Sean O'Neill, Ronan Design

Permissions:
Feldman and Associates

Developed by Nieman Inc.

The editors have made every effort to trace the ownership of all copyrighted selections found in this book and to make full acknowledgment for their use. Omissions brought to our attention will be corrected in a subsequent edition.

Author/Title Index